What people are saying about ...

THE TRUEST THING

ABOUT YOU

"The truth hurts, the phrase goes, but Dave Lomas shows how the truest truth blesses and heals. Read this book and be reminded—or hear for the first time—that you are beloved. Trust it is true, and love will change your life. Enjoy Lomas's masterful fusion of pastoral compassion, writerly wit, and spiritual sincerity."

Jenell Paris, professor of anthropology at Messiah College and author of *The End of Sexual Identity*

"Dave Lomas is hitting on one of the great felt needs of our generation by asking this transformative question: what is the truest thing about you? His perspective on identity is truly needed, flipping the entire subject on its head and driving to the center of who we are as people and ultimately as leaders. Is it what you do? Is it what you're good at? Is it who you know? The answer is so much bigger than these things. I urge you not to miss this important book!"

Brad Lomenick, author of *The Catalyst Leader* and president and key visionary of Catalyst

"Dave Lomas is not only a great pastor and author but a great friend. Over the last few years my heart has been broken beyond my wildest imagination as I watched my young daughter die of cancer. There were times that I would not have made it through if Dave was not there to shepherd my soul with the same great wisdom, insight, compassion, and incisive truth that overflows in this book. I am so thankful for him and the way that this book will serve to heal and propel so many into the mission of Christ."

Britt Merrick, pastor and
author of *Godspeed*

"In *The Truest Thing about You*, David Lomas deftly reveals the dignity of humanity and the freeing reality that the meaning of our lives does not flow from what we do but who we are. So who are we? Read his book and find out. You'll be very glad you did."

Stasi Eldredge, bestselling author of
Becoming Myself and coauthor of *Captivating*

"We live in a world where it is so incredibly easy for what we think about ourselves to be subtly and sometimes not so subtly shaped by culture, people, and our own insecurities. *The Truest Thing about You* is a compass and a map that will help us see how we may have missed the incredible way God created us and how He sees us, which is our true identity. Too many people live their lives not understanding what Dave writes about here. What a joy it is to think about how people's lives will radically change if they grasp the truths within this book."

Dan Kimball, pastor of Vintage Faith and author of *They Like Jesus But Not the Church*

"*The Truest Thing about You* is an important book. It's important because it cuts to the core of what it means to be human, what it means to be loved by God, and what it means to be a disciple of Jesus. And this is not just theory. Dave writes from deep experiences pastoring in one of America's most identity-rich cities. Rarely has a book gotten to the heart of the issue with such precision and skill. I believe this will be a powerful tool for helping people be more transformed into the image of Jesus."

Jon Tyson, lead pastor at Trinity Grace Church in New York

"There are many books on identity but few like this. Here we are told to not only look at the truth of who we are in Christ but to ponder it. Winsome yet bold, Dave's voice is a rare gift that speaks not only for a renewed perspective on identity but from it. His are words that our conflicted world desperately needs to hear."

Tim Chaddick, author of *Better*

"One of the most important things about someone is what they think when they gaze into a mirror and ask, 'Who am I?' The answer to this question shapes what one believes about life and God, purpose and possibility. In *The Truest Thing about You*, Dave Lomas spit shines our mirrors, wiping away the smudges left by insecurities and pains and personal failures. If you've ever felt deflated or discouraged by who you think you are, this book will give you the courage to look again. It will help you to throw off the lies you've come to believe and glimpse a truer and more beautiful image of yourself. Trust me—you can't afford to miss this book."

Jonathan Merritt, author of *Jesus Is Better than You Imagined*

"We are a generation haunted by the question *who am I?* More than ever before, we wander through life confused and lost amid the panoply of options. In a cultural milieu of one identity crisis after another, Dave Lomas's first book comes as firm ground under our feet. Dave is a friend I know and respect. He's smart, humble, kind, self-effacing—and *he has something to say.* I encourage you to listen up."

John Mark Comer, pastor for teaching and vision at Bridgetown: a Jesus Church in Portland, OR, and author of *Loveology.*

"This is not a self-help book, and it won't help you 'find' your identity. It will do far more. Dave's poignant message strikes hard at one of the central chords in our culture—and resonates. All at once a reality check and a paradigm shift, this book is a mirror reflecting back the truest image of each person who dares look into its pages. I think you, like me, will be changed by what you see."

Allison Trowbridge, coauthor of
Godspeed with Britt Merrick

"Books that combine powerful biblical insights with very personal narratives that touch my own mind and heart deeply are rare. Dave Lomas has done that in *The Truest Thing about You*. As you read, you will discover how to form a Jesus-based identity in our world. What a gift Dave has given people seeking truth."

Gerry Breshears, PhD, Western
Seminary, Portland

"My husband and I are missionaries who run a counter human-trafficking NGO out of Cape Town, South Africa, and I am so incredibly thankful for how God has spoken into our lives and ministry through Dave Lomas's teaching. Through him, God has provided answers I had been seeking not only for myself but for some of the people I do life with. Every week I hang out with girls who are in prostitution. All of these girls have given their lives to Jesus, but as Dave wrote about his church, they are 'still sinning.' I felt like I never had the language to communicate to them what I wanted to share, never had the words to express how they could take the next steps in their journey with God, but through Dave's message I sensed that God was giving me those answers. So thank you, Dave, on behalf of the Capricorn prostitutes and for the impact that I am sure every one of them will have on the kingdom of God. And on a personal level, thank you for what your words and the Holy Spirit have worked in my own heart: new passions and new freedom to live in fullness."

Kimberly Brune, Justice ACTs
International Coordinator

THE

TRUEST

THING

ABOUT

YOU

THE

IDENTITY.

TRUEST

DESIRE.

THING

AND WHY

ABOUT

IT ALL MATTERS.

YOU

DAVID LOMAS

WITH D.R. JACOBSEN

David C Cook®
transforming lives together

THE TRUEST THING ABOUT YOU
Published by David C Cook
4050 Lee Vance View
Colorado Springs, CO 80918 U.S.A.

David C Cook Distribution Canada
55 Woodslee Avenue, Paris, Ontario, Canada N3L 3E5

David C Cook U.K., Kingsway Communications
Eastbourne, East Sussex BN23 6NT, England

The website addresses recommended throughout this book
are offered as a resource to you. These websites are not
intended in any way to be or imply an endorsement on the
part of David C Cook, nor do we vouch for their content.

All Scripture quotations, unless otherwise noted, are taken from the
Holy Bible, New International Version®, NIV®. Copyright © 1973, 2011
by Biblica, Inc.™ Used by permission of Zondervan. All rights reserved
worldwide. www.zondervan.com. Scripture quotations marked NASB are
taken from the New American Standard Bible®, Copyright © 1960, 1995
by The Lockman Foundation. Used by permission. (www.Lockman.org.)
The author has added italics to quotations for emphasis.

LCCN 2013955965
ISBN 978-0-7814-0855-4
eISBN 978-0-7814-1127-1

© 2014 David Lomas, D. R. Jacobsen
Published in association with the literary agency of D.C. Jacobson
& Associates LLC, an Author Management Company
www.dcjacobson.com

The Team: Alex Field, Nicci Hubert, Amy Konyndyk,
Nick Lee, Caitlyn Carlson, Karen Athen
Cover Design: Dann Petty

Printed in the United States of America
First Edition 2014

1 2 3 4 5 6 7 8 9 10

112613

To Ashley.
My sunshine. My moonlight.

CONTENTS

Author's note:

Reader,

This is not a traditional foreword. I asked my friend Francis to read my book and think about writing the foreword to it. He wrote me the following letter in response. We were going to change it so it sounded more typical ... until we both realized that his letter was already perfect for the job. I hope you enjoy reading over my shoulder.

Grace, peace,
Dave

FOREWORD
BY FRANCIS CHAN

Dave,

I have such a fear of leaving the earth without leaving an impact, and that can cause me to run frantically from task to task. I get busy doing everything I think I need to do, and I forget to thank God for what He has already done. I often work mindlessly, rather than letting my actions spring from the deep enjoyment of being God's child.

Looking back, I can see how I've tried to get others to perform, regardless of their motivation. I've focused a lot on their *work* and not enough on their *identity*. In hindsight, I realize I was shooting myself in the foot. I was trying to squeeze Christ-like actions out of people who hadn't been transformed by Christ. You've helped me remember that when we trust in Christ, and take hold of that identity, our actions begin to happen naturally—or supernaturally.

This may be a corny illustration, but I think about the Gatorade commercial where they ask, "Is it in you?" It shows athletes literally sweating Gatorade out of their pores. The point is that since Gatorade is inside of them, it naturally pours out. This resonates with what Scripture teaches. God promises an internal change that takes place in those who believe, and then godly actions pour out of us as a result. That makes us ask: if the actions aren't naturally pouring out ... is God in you?

It's the good tree that can't help but bear good fruit.[1] It's out of the overflow of the heart that the mouth speaks.[2] It's God's promise to change our hearts of stone to hearts of flesh.[3] And it's because God put His Spirit in us that we hate evil and love what is right.[4]

Once this internal change takes place, it's as if we can't stop ourselves from acting. That's how the Christian life is supposed to work. Something wells up inside us and then overflows. We *have* to love God. We *have* to serve God. We *have* to love people … not because we're supposed to, but because we can't help it! We don't try to love the poor—we can't help but love the poor! We *want* to. It's flowing out of every fiber of our being. We hate lust and pride and try to rid ourselves of them, not because we're supposed to be good, but because those things aren't who we are. When we're filled with God, His commands aren't burdensome—we actually love them! He makes us slaves of righteousness,[5] and we love it!

Thank you for reminding me to dwell on the promises of Scripture. I'm guilty of ignoring those promises, and it often leads to pride or discouragement. So many of us grew up in homes where we never felt secure. We had to work extra hard, trying to earn approval or love that never came. Our tendency is to carry that mind-set into our relationship with God. We end up anxiously working to gain approval, not realizing that we already possess it.

Thank you for taking the time to articulate what the Lord has taught you in this area. I believe it will help many and bring glory to God. Personally, I believe I will become a better pastor, dad, and lover of God because of it. People like me need a book like this. I pray that my lifestyle changes in light of what I have just read.

I love you, brother. I knew God introduced us a few years ago for a reason. I thought it was so we could "do" something together, like "bring revival to SF!" But I see now that it was to enjoy the revival He's already given us. I still believe we will see great things happen in the future, but it will be the result of you and me living out our identity as a couple of God's beloved kids.

Thank you for writing this book.

Your friend,
Francis

WHO WE ARE
A COLLECTION OF SOMEONES

*You find peace not by rearranging the circumstances of
your life, but by realizing who you are at the deepest level.*

Eckhart Tolle

TRUER THINGS

There are many true things about you. You may be a student.
You may be a mom. You may love someone of the opposite
sex or the same sex. You may make music or lattes. Life may be
incredibly difficult, or you may feel like you're living the dream.

These things may be true—but are they the *truest*?

Fried chicken is food, true, and so is a kale salad. But Jesus declared that He is the truest food. See, other things may have the appearance of being able to satisfy the deep needs of our bodies and even our souls, but Jesus declared that He is even *truer food* and *truer drink*.[1]

So even among truths, there are true things and there are truer things.

This book is about the truer things, the things so deeply true about you that they have the power to change everything else, including the merely true things.

What if the truest thing about you can cause you to reimagine your entire life? What if the truest thing about you can drown out all the noise and speak the words that you've waited for your whole life?

Amid all the true things about you, there is one thing that is the truest.

What we are going to attempt to discover is this: what does *God* say is the truest thing about us?

We aren't always comfortable asking that question, and sometimes we only pretend to ask it. We give an answer we think we ought to give, an answer that identifies us as one of the good kids or a good Christian or a good citizen. Those answers are too easy. They're cheap. All our lives we've been trained to answer that question in particular ways for particular people.

We define ourselves differently to different people. I'm a good worker, I'm a good parent, I'm a failure, I'm beautiful, I'm hideous, I'm loved, I'm not.

And maybe you answer the question differently when you're by yourself, when you ask it of yourself. Dancing alone, driving alone, sitting at a café alone, tapping snooze on your alarm for the seventh time, the tenth time, because there isn't one single reason you can come up with for getting out of bed on a sunny Saturday in June.

You answer it differently every time because you feel different every time you're asked. A different person with every shifting truth.

Here's the problem: you're clinging to true things about yourself that simply aren't *that* true. You're elevating things that are merely true—or half-true, or true some days but not others—to the level of "truest." I know you're doing this because I do it too. We all do. It's the human condition.

Be clear: many of the destructive things we believe about ourselves are *not*, in fact, lies.

Well-intentioned people sometimes tell us not to believe lies about ourselves. They tell us that we can put negative thoughts behind us and begin to live positive lives.

That's missing the point though. There are many destructive things about us that aren't lies we need to reject. In fact, many destructive things we believe are very much true! We *do* fail, we *did* lose the money, we *aren't* as beautiful, we *were* abused. The problem is that we have pushed many of these merely true things down to the most fundamental layer of who we are and in so doing have built our whole lives and identities on them.

These things can be true, but we need to discover that they are not, and never will be, the *truest* thing.

That's what this book is about.

WHY IT MATTERS

Have you ever realized that the most fundamental and existential questions in life spring from your identity?

Who am I?

Why am I here?

What am I meant to be?

What is my purpose?

Can I ever change who I am?

Does anyone know and love the real me?

These are the kinds of questions that keep us up at night—or else they are so troubling that we watch movies, work over-time, stay out late, get high, or try to lose ourselves in romance just to avoid asking them.

If one of the most important aspects of your life has ever changed, you know exactly what I'm talking about. Maybe once upon a time your job was everything. You worked long hours, but it didn't feel like work because you were a part of something. Something big. You had power, you had money, you had purpose. Perhaps you loved the certainty that everyone needed you or that you were making a real difference.

Or you had that relationship everyone really wants. You never dreamed that you could be so happy or that another person could get you at such a deep level. You were fulfilled.

Perhaps you were your parents' favorite child, home for every holiday and loving every minute. You always knew who you were, and you always knew you were loved.

Then one day you woke up ... and it was all gone. I see this happen all the time. It's happened to me on several occasions. You were fired, laid off when your company downsized, or, worse, you simply felt bored and left. That relationship ended bitterly, or you were blindsided by the loss of your parents. Who you were was no longer who you would be. All of those questions you'd been managing to avoid came boiling to the surface again. The way it happens can be different, but it still happens to each of us.

It's been said that our identity is that which is identical about us in every situation. Identity. Identical.

Yet that doesn't help much because we are composite people, bundles of competing desires and identities. We want to be educated thinkers and we want to watch reality television. We want to be generous and we want our own way every time. We want to be in shape and we want to eat bacon! But if the basic conflicts in our natures are obvious, then so is our sense, our intuition, that beneath all that oscillation is a stable core of identity. Somewhere inside us is who we *really* are.

How do we get to that core identity? What happens when we feel like we're constantly in flux, unable to identify *anything* that's always the same about us? Or what happens when we feel exactly the same as everyone else, just another cog in the machine with no individual spark?

On one level, the feeling of constant change has become constant. When switching apartments and jobs and cities and cars and friends and churches is normal, so is our feeling of déjà vu. We've been here before. We've done that, met them, seen this. Change, change, change—and before long we feel like a well-used Rubik's Cube, always spinning but getting more and more random each time.

On another level, some things about us are so permanent that their weight feels crushing. Our ethnicity, our past crimes and failures, our families, our disorders and addictions. There's no way we can escape such things.

That's why we are so conflicted, because so many competing and complementary things about us are true at the same time. We can hate that which is permanent about ourselves, like the way we were raised, just as we can hate that which is temporary, like a bad haircut. We're after something deeper, some truer identity that makes sense of our myriad parts.

Princeton professor Kwame Anthony Appiah pointed out that identity is a combination of how we represent ourselves to ourselves and how the world sees us. He said we are always navigating between the "I" in "I am ..." and the "me" people see as being *me*.

That balancing act poses some obvious problems, some of which Professor Appiah highlighted. What if the "I" you want to be known as is quite different from the "me" that people see? In my own life I might ask, *What if people see me as Mexican, but I want to be seen as Asian?* Or, *What if people see me as a pastor, but I want to be seen as a creative writer?*

My wife has this existential crisis every time she introduces herself to someone in our church community. She doesn't want to be seen as "the pastor's wife" or "the first lady" (ha!)—she wants to be seen as Ashley. Just her. But she *is* the pastor's wife. She knows that and loves that on one level, but that truth brings expectations of having it all together, running the kids' program and women's ministry at the same time, discipling every girl in the church, and being the woman Solomon said in the ancient book of Proverbs was the ideal.[2]

There's a way she sees herself—and there is a way others see and interpret her. She needs to navigate her "I" and the "me" that others see.

So is identity that which is most identical about you in all situations? Even if some of those identical things change and some regrettably stay the same?

Or is identity what you want to be seen as and how the world sees you? And can you change to be anything you want?

These questions matter—a lot—because our identity is the lens through which we see the world. We cannot *not* see our lives—lives sometimes magnificent in detail and beauty, other times crushing in blurriness and drab normality—from the perspective of who we believe we are. Our identity shapes the way we live.

I read this illustration once: identity drives motivation, motivation drives action, and action drives results. For example, if someone speeds past me at ninety miles per hour on the highway, odds are I won't chase them down and issue a ticket. I don't have an identity that says, "I am a police officer," so I have no motivation to act. A police officer, on the other hand, does have that identity and therefore has the motivation to take action (chasing down the speeder) and get results (issuing a ticket).[3]

Every action we take in life has a sense of identity behind it. How we see ourselves matters.

So who is that? What *is* the truest thing about you? What part of you is unchangeable? Who are you?

You're a mom. A dad. A child of divorce. A business owner or freelancer. Male, female, black, white. You're an introvert, an extrovert, a person who refuses to be labeled as either. You're gay, you're straight. You're a success, a failure, someone who never lived up to other people's expectations, or someone no one ever believed in. You control your own destiny or you cannot seem to escape the labels other people give you.

Unique among seven billion other options, you are you—but who *is* that? What does it mean to be you, and what if you don't like the answer?

We don't have midlife crises anymore. We live in perpetual crisis.

The constant crisis can wear us down. Identity isn't something we can safely ignore until we get a raise or the kids are in school full-time or we retire. No—*who we believe we are determines how we live our lives each day.* That is why all this matters.

When it comes to our identity, to the truest thing about us, we can't afford to believe partial truths. Even worse, sometimes we believe lies. Sometimes I still do. I wrote this book because I needed to read it, needed to believe it.

I *still* need to believe it.

If discovering the truest thing about who we are is a journey, we're all taking it together.

ME

My identity crisis started way before midlife—at least I hope.

I'm from Bakersfield, a town in the central valley of California. It's nowhere near the beach, and you never run into movie stars. You do meet growers, people who work in oil, and educators. The nearest forest is actually neatly ordered almond and olive groves, and the nearest river is lined with cement. Bakersfield doesn't have any sports teams, but the Lakers do play one preseason game there every year, or at least they used to. On an electoral map of blue California, Bakersfield is a bright red splotch smack in the middle of the state. I was born there, graduated from high school there, met Jesus and my wife there, and became a pastor at a church there.

Now I live in San Francisco, and the church I started is in the middle of the Castro District. On an electoral map, San Francisco (especially the Castro District) is so blue it glows. San Francisco is 282 miles from Bakersfield, but the distance might as well be measured in light-years.

Between Bakersfield and San Francisco is a quaint beach town on California's Central Coast called Carpinteria. The postcards they sell at the local steak house, The Palms, are right—it really is "The Promised Land." I moved to Carpinteria because I believed God was asking me to start a new church community, and moving away from Bakersfield was the first step. It was in that town nestled comfortably between the Santa Ynez Mountains and the cool Pacific that my identity imploded.

I was thirty. I'd just started working at Starbucks. And my boss had just graduated ... from high school.

In Bakersfield, I'd been on staff at a church for nearly a decade. People called me Pastor Dave. People came to me for help with major decisions in their lives, like marriage and career changes. I prayed with people and taught them about the Bible and helped students keep their eyes on what mattered during their years in school. And I loved every minute of it.

At Starbucks, people called me "man" and asked me why there wasn't more caramel syrup on their latte. People wanted my help with major decisions like which scone to buy. Not that baristas don't add value to people's lives—this book wouldn't have been written without my friendly baristas in San Francisco! But the reality was that I was putting pastries into paper bags and cleaning bathrooms *at the same time my whole sense of identity was still wrapped up in being a pastor.*

That cognitive dissonance—and heart dissonance—was at the center of my identity crisis.

....

So why was I working at Starbucks? Because the bank I had been working at prior to Starbucks fired me a week before Christmas. I shouldn't have been surprised. Counting things isn't one of my strengths. (My wife handles the finances at home, and my executive pastor handles the money at our church, so don't be alarmed.) At this bank I kept giving people too much money—no joke. This wasn't me being a gospel-centered banker ... it was me being a *bad* banker. When I worked there, I always wondered why I had the longest line and why people waited to work with me when other tellers were open. At the time I figured it was my charm. Nope.

Fired from the bank, working at Starbucks, and thinking longingly back to my ten years as a respected pastor in my hometown, all while I was preparing to go begin a new church, *somewhere*, with no Bible degree, no seminary training, and about one-third of a community-college transcript.

That was me.

Did I mention that right before the bank fired me I heard God tell me—and it was the clearest voice I'd ever heard—that my wife and I were supposed to move to San Francisco and start a church?

San Francisco. One of the most unchurched, most educated, most culturally progressive cities in the nation. Me, Bakersfield Dave. I had plenty of time to contemplate the absurdity of that call after getting fired from my entry-level banking job and while foaming milk at Starbucks.

Cue identity crisis.

TRUE AND TRUEST

When it comes to an identity crisis, the shift from swimming to drowning isn't always sudden. Major life changes can be as traumatic to our sense of identity as a shark attack … but sometimes all it takes is the hint of a cramp or the tug of a current.

Losing the sense of who we are can be as subtle as waking up and feeling like everything has moved an inch to the left. We're living the same life: same job, same relationships, same parents. Except it's no longer quite the same. Something has changed. A crack, a discordant note. A different quality of light that doesn't seem as promising, as hopeful. Work begins to feel more like work, lovers seem more like friends, the sense of possibility more like expectation.

You knew who you were, and those things that made you *you* were everything—until they weren't.

Did you squander them? Were they taken from you? Was it fate? I'm not going to answer the *why* here because the *what* is painfully, inevitably, humanly universal. These things happen to us all.

If you don't know the truest thing about yourself, you don't know yourself. And that matters. What you believe about yourself determines how you live. We were made for something.

Something bigger than the little things we seem fated to surround ourselves with.

Understanding identity is an act of hope. We *want* to know who we really are because we believe that knowledge will make a real difference in how we live.

It's also difficult, and not just because of the issues that it will raise inside your heart and mind. Some of what we talk about might offend you. This discussion might make you uncomfortable or even disrupt the way you see other people. If you have a habit of being quick to place people into categories of right and wrong, holy and profane, then what I hope is that you will first examine yourself.

Take a vacation from worrying about others. What's *your* identity?

2

HOW WE GOT HERE
A PARADIGM

*Do not let your happiness depend on
something you may lose.*

C. S. Lewis, *The Four Loves*

Let's begin by drilling down into identity—exactly how do we become who we are? In Jonathan Franzen's novel *Freedom*, one of the characters, Joey Berglund, reflects that contemporary selfhood can feel like being "a collection of contradictory potential someones."[1]

That's what we are today. A collection of contradictory some-ones, defined by what we do, the things we have, and what we desire. Do, have, desire—they can all be true, but none is the truest. Here's how we can be deceived into false identities.

DO

Recently I was in a coffee shop with a few guys I'm discipling. I asked them the following question: what identity in your life currently provides the most powerful dose of self-worth?[2] Around the table were a single guy, a married guy, and a guy who was married with kids—and without exception, we all talked about our careers.

How do we know we're worth something? How do we know we matter? When the check comes in. When we hear "good job." We can find our self-worth in what we *do* and do *well*.

On an episode of *Mad Men*, Don Draper is forced to fire an employee for drinking too much on the job. (Oh, the irony.) However, he wants the employee to sober up and return to the agency, so he gives the man a year's severance pay and tells him to get clean and come back in a year. The conversation takes place in an alley during a rainstorm. And as Draper climbs into a cab, the former employee looks at him desperately and pleads, "If I don't show up to that office on Monday morning, I don't know who I am."

For that man, it's not about the money—his job is about his sense of self-worth and identity.

It's true that we were created to work and work well. That isn't a lie. (And more on that later.) But we've elevated a true thing about ourselves to the truest thing, and that causes problems.

The way I can prove that to you is this: imagine your job going away. Imagine you blow it. Imagine that what you are very good at doing is taken from you or that you fail at it. Would that be a blow to your sense of self-worth?

There is a fundamental difference between who we are and what we do.

In the past, identity and action seemed to be more unified. Do you know anyone with the last name of Smith or Baker or Miller? Guess what their families used to do? Today, however, we move from job to job to job. The latest research tells us that over the last forty years, the average American has worked 6.3 jobs between the ages of eighteen and twenty-five—and many of us have already beat the average![3]

Can you imagine what our last names would be if we still identi-fied ourselves by our professions? Mine, so far, would be Dave Pastorbankerbaristapastorauthor. Yet if we allow our work to be our identity, we might as well keep adding jobs to our names.

And that's exactly what we do! We don't formalize it by chang-ing our names, but we do it nonetheless. We believe that we are what we do.

In the city where I live, many people equate their job with their identity. San Francisco is a working town, even though on any given day you'll find so many people packed in coffee houses, restaurants, and parks that the city can feel like it's on permanent vacation! But the truth is that it's difficult to live in my city without working—and working hard. All the time I meet people who work in finance, start-ups, tech, arts, and medicine, and they define themselves by what they do. Many of them have moved to San Francisco to do their jobs well with some of the best people in the world.

Work can become life, no matter where we live. Work becomes who we are, whether we're running a company or running a household.

That's why it's so easy to get an identity from what we do, because what we do can give us self-worth and value. Value because I'm valuable to my company or organization. Value because I'm valuable to my family. Value because what I do is valuable to my community or customers.

But what happens when we lose our job? Or our creativity runs through a dry spell? What happens when we get injured in our best sport or our kids rebel or the company we started goes bankrupt or we disappoint our parents or God seems distant or someone else comes along who has more skill and creativity and power than we do?

We lose our sense of self.

When you find your identity in what you *do*, your identity will be shaken the moment you change what you do.

What we do is such a powerful way of defining our identity that we can allow ourselves to be defined even in the nega-tive. Many of us simply want to be noticed for once in our lives. And when we find something to do that gets us noticed, we keep on doing that. From the guy who "just can't find the right job" to the grown daughter who drinks too much at every family holiday because she's "the bad one," we all find it easy to believe that what we do and even what we fail to do defines us.

All of this is understandable. Normally what we say we "do" is the activity that takes up most of our time and thought and energy. I'm Dave the pastor, you're so-and-so the artist or analyst or mom or surfer or dropout or whatever, and all of us believe we can rest comfortably in the knowledge that we are what we do.

Imagine you're at a party, meeting someone for the first time. Your host introduces you and leaves. What's the first thing you say? *So, what do you do?*

And *doing* can be great—until you can't do anymore. Those things that can give us worth can also remove worth.

But here's the truth: what we do is not the truest thing about us. Building our identity on the foundation of what we do creates an identity that can crack or break or tumble down at any moment.

HAVE

We are what we have. And that can be good news just as easily as it can be bad news.

We can have a nose for fashion or good deals, an artistic talent, a winning personality, or a knack for delivering good one-liners. We can be the beautiful one, the one everyone wants to date or sleep with or be with.

Or we can have a disability, a difficult lot in life, absent or abusive parents. We can have the kind of looks and personality that makes everyone want to be "just a friend" and nothing more.

We think that the things we have define us. We overidentify with what we have by making what we have the truest thing about us.

I'm not talking about the whole "you think you're poor, but you're really one of the richest people in the world" meme. That's true enough, but that truth usually rolls like water off our backs, perhaps because we *know* it's true but we *feel* like it isn't.

No, when I talk about what we have, I'm talking about the fact that we have parents, a past, a body, possessions, proclivities, a love, former loves, and so on. That's a lot of things to have—is it any wonder we slog through life like we have the world on our shoulders?

The sum of what we have may not be the world, but it's *our* world, and it's plenty for any one person to carry.

What are the effects of this identity structure? As we saw in chapter 1, if we have looks, we need to *keep* our looks. If we have money, we need to have *more* money. And so life becomes about consumption—about never having enough and always trying to have more.

I grew up without having many of the things other people around me had. I wore shoes and clothes that were copies of the name brands—like my Air Jordan knockoffs. I tried to convince myself that those XJ9000s were just as good as the Nikes, except that they were made out of pleather and plastic. And my classmates never tired of reminding me of that fact.

But when I got my first job, and my second job, all of a sudden I realized I could buy what I wanted to buy—name-brand clothes, the latest music, cool furniture. And one day, as I stood in my studio apartment, I looked at my reflection in the mirror and said these words: "If they could see me now!" (I know, cliché, right?)

Here's the point. Growing up I defined my identity by what I didn't have. And as soon as I could afford to buy what I wanted, I began to define myself by what I did have. I purchased an identity for myself.

I wish I could say I stopped doing that when I was twenty-one. But I still do it now. These subtle temptations toward self-identifying are always with us. We all do this. Good people, mature people, Christian people.

Having can be great—until we always want to have more, or until we want to get rid of what we already have.

What we have—or don't have—is not the truest thing about us.

Building our identity on the foundation of what we have means that we'll always be focused on ourselves. A world of self-focused individuals sounds strangely like the world we live in now ... and it's the lonely experience of living in that very world that sends us in search of something truer.

DESIRE

Doing and *having* can make us feel less than the people around us. Inadequate.

There's a third way we identify ourselves though. Desire.

A recent article put it this way: "The true self lies precisely in our suppressed urges and unacknowledged emotions."[4]

The article continues with a statement that both shocks and seems intuitively true: "To find a moment when a person's true self comes out ... one needs to look at the times when people are so drunk or overcome by passion that they are unable to suppress what is deep within them."[5]

So what's the truest thing about you? What's at your unchangeable core? The only way to answer those questions, according to some, is to smash down every wall that you and others have constructed around your identity. Drugs or sex or some other ecstatic experience are the battering rams. Get past your job and hobbies. Get past what you own and what you wish you had. Get past your friends and family. Then, in a final moment of naked honesty, the true you will be revealed.

This is a contemporary paradigm in which we are what we desire. According to this, the real me is the me I keep hidden because of fear or repressed desire or religion or expectations. All I have to do is discover my true desires.

With desire, there is no necessary hierarchy. We can *have* objectively less than our neighbor: fewer square feet, fewer kids, less responsibility at work, less paid vacation time, less in our retirement accounts, less chance to get ahead. And we can *do* objectively less than our neighbor in all the same ways. However, we can *desire* more than anyone.

I know that's true of me. I can always imagine more. My own temptations match what I spend most of my time doing. More people showing up to hear me preach. More respect in the city. More people baptized. That's a preacher's fantasy; your mileage may vary. But each of us has our own fantasies. For every person there is a different outworking, though common themes of acceptance, power, appreciation, and satisfaction emerge.

And the most common theme of all? Desiring more. It reminds me of the quote from the über-rich John D. Rockefeller, who, when asked how much money was enough, replied, "Just a little bit more."

But if we all desire things, desire must be natural. So what's the real problem here? If we sometimes desire the wrong things, and thus find ourselves with the wrong identity, surely all we have to do is desire better things, right?

The real problem isn't with desire, per se. God tells us that He desires. The Bible is full of references to what God desires. Jesus certainly desired things while He lived on earth, and He desires things now. God's Spirit desires. Stalin and Mother Teresa both had desires. Children are born with desires, and we don't stop desiring things even when we're on our deathbeds. So what does that tell us?

That desire can take us only so far. Desiring good is certainly better than desiring evil. But neither the desire for evil *nor* the desire for good can provide us with our true identity.

Recently someone said to me, "I'm a driven, passionate person. I see what I desire, and I go after it. That's just the way God made me, and I have to humbly accept that." I try not to swear too often, since I'm a pastor and all, but I was very tempted. I wanted to tell him, "Hey, God didn't make you a self-absorbed jerk ... you made yourself into that! God, along with the rest of us, is now suffering the consequences."

This guy wants to have everything he desires, but the simple realities of life will prevent that from happening. He wants to follow God, but he wants to control his own destiny; he wants to be humble, but he wants to self-identify as *driven* (which really means self-centered). The contradictions go on and on.

And that demonstrates the mistake the rest of us make just as often as that guy: what we desire cannot be our identity because our desires conflict! We are walking, talking bundles of contradictory desire. We have spiritual, material, sexual, emotional, and relational desires. We want to be healthy and we want to eat whatever tastes delicious. We want to serve God and we want to serve ourselves. We want to have faithful relationships and we want the constant thrill of novelty.

THE TRUEST THING ABOUT YOU 46

When we take *any* one of our strongly felt desires and construct our entire identity around it, we discover that we are making a *part* of who we are into the *whole* of who we are.

This happens with our sexuality when a *desire* turns into an identity statement about who we are. Who we want sexually becomes who we are socially.[6]

But that isn't really the way life is meant to work. One book I read put it this way: "God created sexuality. People created sexual identity."[7] We know this is true because we know how often our desires change, conflict, and just plain don't make sense. We're *told* that identity can be as simple as joining a community that desires the same thing we do, but we know from experience that such communities are fickle and prone to fragmentation.

It's the same with all our desires. There may not be a problem with desiring in and of itself. However, there is a massive problem with defining your identity by what you desire. "Desire makes us act," wrote Ronald Rolheiser, "and when we act what we do will either lead to a greater integration or disintegration within our personalities, minds, and bodies—and to the strengthening or deterioration of our relationship to God, others, and the cosmic world."[8]

Desiring isn't inherently wrong, and in fact it can be great—until our desires conflict or are unfulfilled or are directed toward the wrong objects or become addictions.

What we desire, whether noble or corrupted, is not the truest thing about us. Building our identity on the foundation of what we desire guarantees that our identity will change every time our desires change.

THE END OF SEXUAL IDENTITY

Perhaps no form of desire seems to change our identity as often or as easily as sexual desire.

As Jenell Paris wrote in her insightful book *The End of Sexual Identity*, "Sex is much more than it used to be. Sexual desire is now considered central to human identity, and sexual self-expression is seen by many to be essential for healthy personhood."[9]

Where I live in San Francisco, desire and sexual attraction can give you an *entire* identity: a community, a social life, a political party, and even a predisposed attitude toward religion. People change their entire lives—from where they live and work and go to church all the way down to the smallest details like what restaurants and bars they frequent—when they come out as gay, or return to being straight, or ... well, you get the idea.

I'm not saying that some of this isn't warranted. For decades, the straight community, and especially the *religious* straight community, has made sexual identity the truest thing about

THE TRUEST THING ABOUT YOU 48

someone. If you are heterosexual, have people in your Christian community let you know that they are gay or lesbian? If so, what was the first thing you assumed? That they were a Christian and a follower of Jesus *first* … or did you yourself reinforce the belief that their sexual identity had become the truest thing about them? Too often this is the case.

We've trained people to think this way. Most people I know believe that their sexual attraction—no matter whom it is for—identifies them. In addition, many believe that the identity of "Christian" competes with certain identities grounded in sexuality.

This is wrong.

The truest thing about our identity can never be limited to or fully described by our sexual desires.

Paris phrased it this way: "All sexual identity categories have a common trouble: they tell us what a person wants, sexually, *is an important measure of who a person is.*"[10]

In other words, we think that we are what we desire.

I get it. This is the message we've been receiving for years, both from outside *and* inside the church. We're constantly being told to desire someone different, or less, or more … and only *then* can we have a real relationship with God. If something can prevent us from having a relationship with God, it surely must be the most significant thing about us!

However, when we define our identity by our sexuality, we end up believing things like this: *Since I'm straight, I don't need to think about sexuality at all. Since I'm gay, my sexual identity competes with my spiritual identity. Since I'm single, I can't fully be who God wants me to be. Since I'm questioning my sexuality, my identity as God's beloved is also in question. Since I'm divorced, God thinks about me differently.*[11]

In all of these cases, we're elevating partial truths (and even lies) to the status of the "truest thing about ourselves."

Straight people, for example, can live completely out of step with a Christian vision of purity and love while believing that they have no serious issues with their sexuality because they're sinning in the "Adam and Eve" paradigm. They can believe that their sexuality has two stages: sin management before marriage and automatic purity and satisfaction after. And so they can fail to bring their sexuality under the deeper truth of their identity in Christ, just as they can assume a sense of righteous identity from their "biblical" sexuality.

Gay people, on the other hand, can view the church with the attitude of "move on, there's nothing for you here," and so fail to see, just as heterosexuals do, that there is something even truer about their identities than who they desire. Add to this the fact that our sexual identities seem to be more fluid and subject to change than ever, and it's no wonder we often allow sexual identity categories to define the *entirety* of who we are.

This kills me.

Identity in Christ is truer than *every* other voice we hear. Gay, straight, divorced, lesbian, single, bi, celibate—identity in Christ is true regardless of our attractions. It's truer than our sexual identity labels.

However, American Christians are a pragmatic people. We want answers. We want a formula for how churches should treat the LGBTQ community, or for what people need to do before becoming believers. I recently had a pastor ask me, "What's the best way to welcome everyone to my church— tell them to become straight and then join us?"

No.

But now you're probably thinking, *I know—the real answer is to meet Jesus and then get straight.*

Nope. The real answer is Jesus. Full stop. For *every* person.

As I've pastored people in my church, my sole purpose and goal has been the same with every single one: to help them understand that their fundamental and truest identity is found in Jesus.

What about discipleship? Here's the deal with Jesus. He's egalitarian when it comes to this issue, and He wants *everyone* to repent of their sexuality because *everyone* is broken sexually. Straight, gay, bi, whatever ... if there is something truer to our fundamental identity than Jesus and what it looks like to follow Him, we're not really following Him.

Can we all take down the sign above the church door that says "straight people only" or "gay people only" and put up the sign that says "whosoever"?

The truest thing about you is not what or who you desire any more than it can be what you do or what you have. Your identity is not determined by who you love or have sex with. Those things are true about you, yes, but they can never be the truest.

When you come to Christ, no matter the shape of your desires, you are given a new identity. You are hidden with Christ, and you are the beloved of God. Period. That's the label that supersedes all others.

MOVING ON

Let me lay out some facts as I see them.

There is nothing about what you *do* that is 100 percent secure.

There is nothing about what you *have* that cannot be taken from you.

There is nothing about what you *desire* that cannot change.

Do you disagree with these statements? To me they seem beyond disagreement—not because I'm so wise and pro- found, but because the claims they make seem clear and warranted. As far as I can tell—and I've thought about this a great deal and talked to hundreds of people in all walks of life about this very issue—these three statements are solid, universal descriptions of what it means to be human.

And that's what they are: descriptions. No more, no less.

Descriptions need to be interpreted and understood. Conclusions need to be drawn, lived, and constantly evalu- ated. The rest of the book you're holding tries to do exactly that.

It won't always be easy or clear or cut-and-dried. A pastor I know once said something like, "No pastor lives up to what they preach—if they do, they aren't preaching high enough."

In other words, I need this book. I'm not speaking as someone who is this totally secure guy who always lives out of the truest thing about me. I'm still wrestling with these issues, which is why I'm still preaching the gospel to myself.[12] Daily.

I am convinced that there is nothing we can do or have or desire that can supply our true identity. If that description of human life is true, what's next?

There is a way forward into the truth about identity, but first we must go backward.

Because it was God who created humanity, only God can reveal to us our identity as humans.[13] And so the next part of our story takes us all the way back to the time when our identity was first created, in a perfect garden, and to what happened to shatter that perfection.

3

WHAT WE ARE MEANT TO BE
THE IMAGO DEI

Be who God meant you to be and
you will set the world on fire.

Saint Catherine of Siena

BEGINNINGS

Imago Dei is a religious term that gets a good amount of airtime, and we might even know its definition, but we don't always know what it *means*. However, it is impossible to understand our identity without understanding the meaning of *imago Dei*.

Literally "image of God," *imago Dei* is a Latin term for *tzelem elohim* (zay-LEEM el-oh-HEEM), a Hebrew phrase found in the account of creation in Genesis 1. In the opening pages of Genesis, we see God's direct declaration of the concept. God says to Godself (I know that's confusing, but God has always existed in a relationship between three Persons—Father, Son, Spirit—which we call the Trinity[1]), "Let us make humans in *our image*, in *our likeness*, so that they may rule over the fish in the sea and the birds in the sky, over the livestock and all the wild animals, and over all the creatures that move along the ground."[2]

So what is this saying? God decided to make humanity in His image, after His likeness, and then God gave humanity a job and a vocation, calling humanity into His work of creation care—and it is work that is never done alone.

The story continues: "So God created humans in his own image, in the image of God he created them; *male and female* he created *them*."[3] When we say that God created people in His image, we're pulling language directly out of the first chapter of the Bible, language that describes some essential characteristic that all humans share precisely because they are created by God.

Where it gets complicated is when we try to figure out exactly what it means to be created in God's image.

Is God's image something we have?

Possess?

Demonstrate?

Do we carry it with us wherever we go?

Can we lose it?

Before we get any further, it will be useful to step back from any specific definitions and make a broader point: whatever *imago Dei* means, it must certainly mean it for all people at all times. And whatever it means, it has everything to do with our identity because it is how we were created.

Imago Dei resides in you, and it resides in me. It resides in the brilliance of the most elite medical doctors and in the eyes of the most downtrodden homeless people. And it has since the beginning of human existence.

Yes, it's true that when you read ahead a few chapters in Genesis, things get really bad. In chapter 3, humanity falls. Cornelius Plantinga coined one of my favorite descriptions of what happens: *the vandalism of shalom*. The peace of God (*shalom* in Hebrew), which held everything together in perfect harmony and balance in Genesis 1–2, was defaced and damaged. But here's the question: Did we cease to be human at that point? Did our *fundamental* identity change? I don't think so.[4] I would add that just as we did not lose our humanity, neither did we lose our call. God never took away our call to be both bearers of His image and stewards over His creation.

Imago Dei is for all people at all times. It's who we are.

Let's start there. Our identity begins in how God created us. Maybe all our longings and desires point us back to this ... to how it was meant to be. To how *we* were meant to be.

Genesis, along with other parts of the Bible, has become white noise to many of us. That's unfortunate but true. We think we already know what it means, or else we don't think it means anything to us at all. Perhaps you even skimmed the last few paragraphs as soon as I mentioned Genesis.

I recently sat with some friends who I've been walking through Scripture and life with. We started in Genesis, and I asked, "What does it mean to be created by God?" These guys have been in church for a long time, way before I ever met them. They'd probably heard the garden of Eden story alluded to or taught dozens of times. They, like all of us can be, were inoculated against the power and the truth of it.

Perhaps we have heard Genesis, but do we really *listen* to it? Do we find in it fresh ways to know God and know ourselves?

This is the kind of God-centered reading that helps alert us to the fact that the Bible frequently seems less concerned with our agendas and more concerned with God's. For example, we sometimes want to read Genesis as a scientific treatise proving that the earth is just over six thousand years old, or that the universe is the result of the big bang billions of years ago. Voltaire poked fun at this proclivity when he observed, "If God has made us in his image, we have returned him the favor."

The reality is that Genesis wants to read *us* instead. It's aiming at something different. God, through Genesis, declares that God is powerful, God is good, and God had a specific intention in creating humanity and placing His image within each of us.

If you have time, go back and read Genesis 1–2. Make an effort to throw away what you think Genesis is saying, and instead read it like you're coming to it for the first time *in order to find out who you were created to be*. For it is in Genesis that our identity begins.

THE ENGINE

Let's return to the *imago Dei* and try to discover some of what Genesis might have to teach us about identity. Isn't it true that when we try to identify ourselves, we usually look inward?

Take a good, hard look inside your heart and find yourself, we're told. *Search your heart.*

This isn't wrong; it's simply wrongly ordered. The Bible does indeed ask us to look inside ourselves to discover our identity— but only *after* we look at God and God's creation. Like a rock climber ascending a cliff face, sequence matters. We can't look inside until we know what God has placed there for us to find.

My wife was recently babysitting a young boy. They had a nice dinner and some playtime, and then it was time to get ready for bed. As the boy was lying on his changing table, and my wife leaned over him to put on his pajamas, he noticed something about her face. Freckles. They grace my wife's cheekbones every year when it's sunny enough—for us here in San Francisco, that means October when the sun finally comes out after our cold, foggy summers. This boy had been too young to notice the freckles the previous year, so he was surprised to see them now. Kids aren't shy when it comes to talking about bodies, so he was like, "Where'd you get *freckles*?"

My wife told him, "Well, that's how God made me."

That's when things got deep. The boy took that in, and then he asked, "God made you?"

"Yep, God made me."

"Well, did God make *me*?"

"Yep, God made you, too."

"Well, did God make my mommy and daddy?"

"God made them, too."

My wife was feeling overwhelmed. A normal bedtime interaction had turned into something far more important. She was getting to share with this precious three-year-old about the ultimate things in life, about God and creation and identity and how we're all God's children.

The little boy looked at my wife. Then he stood up, took a deep breath, and started belting out, "All the single ladies, all the single ladies, all the single ladies, all the single ladies ..." while dancing on his changing table.[5]

Moment shattered.

I love that story, but as I've thought about it, I wonder if it isn't a great illustration of what happens when any of us is told that God created us in His image.

To many of us, that sounds like the kind of statement that produces a profound ... yawn. *I'm created in God's image, huh? You don't say—and what should I watch on Netflix tonight?* It's a statement that is at best informational and at worst irrelevant. We quickly move on to the next thing. Either we believe it's true but it has no impact on how we live and think and act or else we think it's nonsense. It falls into the same category of information as chemistry: perhaps useful for a certain specialized class of people, but to us nothing more than something to forget as soon as we move on to more personally relevant information.

However, I believe that we can't "move on" with our lives in any meaningful sense—ever—unless we understand this. Knowing that we are created in God's image isn't an optional add-on that makes our lives a bit nicer. Is life a pretty great car, and knowledge of the *imago Dei* like adding a sunroof or nicer wheels?

No. *Imago Dei* is the engine.

We fall easily into the trap of believing that we are what we do and have and desire because, hardwired into who we are, those things are a part of how we were created. But they have been hijacked, and now they are inordinate. We need to reclaim the primary truth of our created and given identity: as *made in the image of God.*

THE SONG

In Genesis 1, the creation of humans in God's image is the high point of the song of creation.

There's an easy way to tell what the best part is in any story: it's where you slow things down. Way down. If you're the storyteller, you savor the moments. You pause the narrative as you make eye contact with each of your listeners. You smile and use hand gestures and lift your eyebrows. That's the way the best stories are delivered, isn't it? With a sense of drama and pleasure?

That's what happens in the archetypal story of creation as well. The writer of Genesis 1 employs several storytelling tricks—literary devices—to make sure that the climax of the creation story is both noticed and appreciated.

It all starts with pronouns.[6] Seriously. Through the first twenty-six verses of Genesis, as God proceeds to create everything *but* men and women, we read a series of statements that include "God said" and "God saw." These statements follow a pattern: God says He is going to make something, He makes it, and then He sees that it is good. However, when we reach verse 26, a new pronoun is introduced in God's speech, and it signifies a dramatic change:

> Then God said, "Let *us* make humans in our image, in *our* likeness, so that they may rule over the fish in the sea and the birds in the sky, over the livestock and all the wild animals, and over all the creatures that move along the ground."

Only when God created humanity did He refer to His own plurality. Why? I believe it is because humans are unique in all creation.

In the verse preceding the creation of humanity, we read that God made animals according to their kinds, livestock according to their kinds, and all the creatures that move along the ground according to their—wait for it—kinds.

Now if you've been around the evangelical church for any length of time, you'll know that this verse is used by certain Christians to disprove evolution, but that's not what's really going on here. The point of the animals being created "according to their kinds" hinges on what comes directly after that: to show the contrast with how humanity was created.

Animals were created to be like other animals, while humans were created in the *likeness of God*.

Animals were created according to their *kind,* but what *kind* was humanity created after? God.

"Let us make humans in *our* image, in *our* likeness...." In our *kind*.

Not only are we created *by* God, we're created *like* God!

That isn't the only important point waiting for us in this verse. We should also note that God created *humans* in His image, not simply *men*. The text clearly says that humankind (*a'dam* in Hebrew) is male and female, and so both are made in and reflect God's image. Just as the Bible never says that God is a man, it never says that only men bear God's image.

So whatever the *imago Dei* is, we can be sure of a few things: it's present in all people at all times, it's critical, God placed it only in humans—both male and female—and God wanted us to know about it.

Why might that be? Before we go there, we need to look at one more thing.

TRIPTYCH

The church has always had screens at the front of the building— but only recently have we started projecting song lyrics onto them with accompanying videos of eagles in glorious flight.

For 95 percent of church history, "screens" were either drawn, painted, or crafted from colored glass. We're most familiar with stained glass. It almost feels as if our idea of a real church, or at least our idea of an *old* church, requires the presence of stained glass. Church architecture, at least until recent times, was carefully crafted to communicate the gospel and stir feelings of praise and awe in worshippers. Stained glass told the Bible's stories to illiterate people, and it reminded even literate people of the power of some of those stories. Stained glass also demonstrated that artistic talent, when used to create cultural objects that honor God, is part of the *imago Dei*.

A type of "screen" equally common in church history, though less well known, was paintings. Serving essentially the same function as stained glass, paintings had the added virtue of being portable and harder to break. One specific and fascinating type of sacred painting was the *triptych* (trip-tick). Patterned after the word *diptych*, meaning "folded twice," a triptych was a painting with three sections on hinges that could be closed when not in use. If you've ever done a middle-school science project and pasted your earth-shattering findings on a three-part poster board—*Baking soda and vinegar are sort of like lava! Houseplants like water better than Pepsi!*—you've created a triptych. In the Middle Ages, a nameless Christian farmer in rural France may have lived a pretty dull life in terms of color and artistry, but every Sunday morning he could look forward to the opening of his church's bright and beautiful triptych.

The first triptych actually occurred all the way back in the first chapter of Genesis. Here's what it says:

> So God created humans in his own image,
>   in the image of God he created them;
>   male and female he created them.[7]

Remember how we looked at the literary devices the writer of Genesis used, how things slow down, how the poetry of the moment is allowed to unfold, how there is an accretion of drama that steadily builds to a pinnacle of importance?

Here, in verse 27, we can picture a triptych being opened—and this particular work of art was created by none other than the original Creator. If the preceding verses are the sanctuary, this verse is the moment a beautiful secret is revealed to all the worshippers hungry for light and goodness and a reminder of what is true.

It is a three-part truth: we are created beings, we are made in God's image, and this is true of both male and female.

You may be wondering why we've been talking about art for so long—what does this have to do with identity? I want you to consider this: every human life has equal dignity and worth because Genesis 1:27 is true. That, friends, is a very big deal.

Every human endeavor to protect the vulnerable, disenfranchised, and oppressed—including the American civil rights movement, women's suffrage, the movement to end abortion, and efforts toward clean water—has its roots in a belief that a human person is fundamentally valuable and consequently has certain rights that are wrong to deny. Similarly, every human movement toward repression and totalitarianism—from communism to Sharia law to fascism—grows in the soil of ignorance or intentional dehumanization that suggests certain humans matter more and are more valuable than other humans.

God works differently.

In Genesis 9:5, God warned Noah and his sons that "for your lifeblood I will surely demand an accounting ... [and] from each human being, too, I will demand an accounting for the life of another human being." In other words, we can't choose to dispose of a human life any way we want, because every human is created in God's image. In a direct correlation, we hurt God when we hurt another person.

It works the other way too. For example, in Matthew 25, Jesus told the parable of the sheep and the goats. In this story, the righteous and the unrighteous are separated by what they have done—or left undone—for the impoverished, sick, and imprisoned. The ones who have acted on behalf of those vulnerable persons are called righteous, while the ones who ignored those vulnerable persons—and thus ignored their *imago Dei*—are called unrighteous.

Jesus was blunt: "Whatever you did for one of the least of these brothers and sisters of mine, you did for me."[8]

Every person—body, mind, soul—has inherent worth. No person is worth more than any other person in an absolute sense. Are we all broken? Yes—but we are *all* broken. "For *all* have sinned and fall short of the glory of God,"[9] wrote the apostle Paul, yet God "wants *all* people to be saved."[10] We are both wonderfully created and terribly flawed. All of us. No *individual* has a special claim to God's love because *all* have a special claim to God's love.

Though distorted by sin, the image of God present in every person is the foundation upon which any meaningful project of human rights must necessarily be built. One of my friends started a ministry in a district in San Francisco that few people even know is a part of the city. It's full of gangs, drugs, and violence and is home to middle schoolers who carry guns because Mom and Grandma won't let them leave the house without protection. When my friend tells these people's stories to me, his heart is broken, and my heart breaks as well. Why? Because they are made in the image of God, just like everyone else.

What does this all mean? It means you have worth because you are made in the image of God. You matter to God. No matter your past, no matter your proclivities, your habits, your flaws, your temptations, your orientation. You have worth! You are not what you do. Your self-worth does not depend on what you have. You are not a prisoner of what you desire. No—what the Scriptures make clear is this: humans, created by God, are a finite, visible picture of the infinite, invisible God.

So this is the Genesis key: we don't find our identity.

That runs counter to the stream of our culture, but it is an undeniable biblical truth. *We don't find our identity.*

Rather, we *receive* our identity. We are given it by God. Everything true about our identity is true because it was created and gifted to us by God.

That is why our self-worth derives from the act of our creation. We are rooted in the *imago Dei*. You are. I am. The weird smelly guy who sleeps in the armchair at your favorite Starbucks is. Every single person who has ever lived reflects and represents the everlasting God who created the universe and everything in it. That's the *imago Dei*.

If you have the slightest doubt about this, take your Bible to the beach or the mountains or your backyard at night and read Psalm 8.

> LORD, our Lord,
>> how majestic is your name in all the earth!
>
> You have set your glory
>> in the heavens.
> Through the praise of children and infants
>> you have established a stronghold
>>> against your enemies,
>> to silence the foe and the avenger.
> When I consider your heavens,
>> the work of your fingers,
> the moon and the stars,
>> which you have set in place,
> what is mankind that you are mindful of them,
>> human beings that you care for them?
>
> You have made them a little lower than the angels

and crowned them with glory and honor.
You made them rulers over the works of your
hands;
you put everything under their feet:
all flocks and herds,
and the animals of the wild,
the birds in the sky,
and the fish in the sea,
all that swim the paths of the seas.

LORD, our Lord,
how majestic is your name in all the earth!

Notice the Genesis song being sung again. You are created by God! *Imago Dei*, given glory and honor. Given a mandate to care for the work of creation. We are created—all of us, male and female, old and young, all races and creeds and languages—and we carry with us, all of the time, God's image.

Let the truth of that triptych unfold in your mind. Let the image fill you.

LIVING LIKENESSESS

To be created in God's image means you have worth. I don't claim to know what you have gone through in life, but I know no matter what it's entailed, inside of you is the *imago Dei*. At the root of that *imago Dei* is this reality: *we are created—and created for community and culture.* (I know—three Cs. I'm a preacher. That's how we roll.)

Let's unpack. No matter how independent you or I may feel, at our core we are *created* beings. Nearly every identity issue begins with the misconception that we are not dependent and created—we love to pretend that we are "self-made." Remember, we don't find or even make an identity. We receive one.

Acts 17:28 captures this truth with one of the more stunning images in Scripture. Paul, preaching about the resurrected Christ, hijacked a contemporary poet and said that it's actually in Jesus that "we live and move and have our being." Now think about the word picture Paul was painting: Jesus is like the air we breathe—He's *that* essential to our lives. And since we don't usually consider the air we breathe on a daily basis, let's recast the metaphor a bit. We are fish, and Jesus is the water in which "we live and move and have our being." If you're a fish, you are absolutely helpless without water.

So the Scripture reveals that this Jesus—the cosmic, resurrected Christ—is the One on whom we are dependent. And this isn't a new reality; it's the way life has been all along. Look at John 1: "In the beginning was the Word, and the Word was with God, and the Word was God. He was with God in the beginning. Through him all things were made; without him nothing was made that has been made. In him was life, and that life was the light of all."[11]

All things. There is not a single solitary scrap of reality that was made without Christ, and there is not a second that ticks by without Christ's active, sovereign sustaining. We are created, yes, but not created and then left to our own devices. We are planned, created, and sustained. There isn't a good word for this depth of createdness; if we were talking in person I would look you in the eye, perhaps grab your shoulder to press home the point, and say, "You are *created.*"

This is where you must draw your self-image, self-worth, and value: in all of your created creatureliness.

But created for what? To paraphrase the *Westminster Shorter Catechism*, you were created for the purpose of glorifying God and enjoying Him forever. True. Absolutely true. But ... what does that *look* like?

In Genesis we find a report of one of the first things that was "wrong" with creation—trip out on that! God created everything and called it good, yet something was not good enough.

"It is not good for the man to be alone."[12]

So we were created in, and created for, *community.* You need other people. If you don't think so, you're denying something so fundamental to your humanity that I would say you've lost your grip on reality. In any case, I don't think you'd be reading this book if you thought the truest thing about you was that you didn't need anyone else in your life.

The human longing for companionship is on display in our popular culture, featuring in countless songs and movies and books. The speaker in Simon & Garfunkel's "I Am a Rock" tries desperately hard to convince himself that he doesn't need companionship, but he certainly doesn't convince the listener. "A rock feels no pain / and an island never cries,"[13] he sings, yet it's the obvious irony in the claim that gives the song its poignancy and even pain.

Now, have you ever noticed that what happens in the Genesis account of creation sounds like a non sequitur? God tells Adam that it's not good for him to be alone, to which Adam could have replied, "But I have You, God!" Then—and here's where it gets strange—God asks Adam to name the animals! How does *that* add up?

I think the answer is found at the end of Genesis 2:20, which says, "But for Adam no suitable helper was found."

Naming the animals proved conclusively that there was no one like Adam. It was probably during that task that Adam felt all alone in the world—he felt his lack of community and true companionship. If Adam was created in the image of the triune, communal God, how could he reflect that image alone?

How can we?

Adam couldn't fulfill his function as an image bearer without Eve. We are all created for community with God and with our fellow creatures, and that hardwiring for companionship is part of what it means to be image bearers of God.

You can't become who you are all alone. You need people. The truest thing about you isn't all about *you*. It's about God, and it's about others. Eugene Peterson once said that friendship, esteemed by our ancestors, has fallen on hard times among us moderns. It's deep friendships, like the one David had with Jonathan, that are "the most necessary for realizing who we are, for becoming ourselves (and letting others become themselves) with no strings attached."[14]

And what is all this hardwired need for community *for*? In large part to make culture. Theologians refer to it as our *cultural mandate*, but this sounds more complicated than it is. Basically it means that no matter what profession we find ourselves in—no matter what we *do*—we live by a different set of rules. Whether we're raising kids, banking, making sculptures, studying, or practicing law, we see ourselves being sent into our jobs as stewards of the time, talents, and resources that God has endowed and gifted us with.

Culture, simply, is what happens when humans live together, from the smallest village to the most sprawling city. And God-directed culture *making* is simply what happens when we contribute to our families and society. It's what happens when we are honest, when we're kind to strangers, when we honor the dignity of the simplest job, and when we look for opportunities to serve others.

So the *imago Dei* isn't some abstract or irrelevant idea—it's a *way of life* that leads us back to the garden, to the way we were created, as well as forward into the truest thing about us.

COLLECTIVE MEMORIES

J. R. R. Tolkien once wrote of an ache we all experience—the "joy beyond the walls of the world, poignant as grief."[15]

Have you ever felt that?

I have.

On a beautifully mild October evening, my wife and I were married in the garden of an art gallery in our hometown. We'd known each other for nine years, dating for almost the whole time. Before Ash joined me at the altar, I remembered the first time we met. I was sixteen, and after that day all I wanted to do in life was marry her.

It was dusk. I'd picked out the song she would walk down the aisle to: James Taylor's "Something in the Way She Moves." She appeared. And she was beautiful—not just physically, but in the way I could see her heart inside her smile. The way I could see that the tears sliding down her cheeks were made of delight.

And something pierced my heart.

It was a feeling that was nearly all joy, yet commingled with a clear sense of time's passing, of incompleteness, and, yes, even of sadness. This had nothing to do with Ash ... and everything to do with being human. I was beginning to learn that there are moments in life that can last only a moment. That early October evening, even though I knew it was impossible, I wanted to bottle the feeling. I wanted to preserve it on a shelf forever. The way she looked. They way she smelled. Even her tears.

Why are such times ephemeral? And why do we cry? I believe such moments exist when our deepest joy points directly toward something beyond that joy, something so complete that it will make our small joys pale in comparison. Because we intuit this, the best moments in our lives are tinged with sadness. We know that those moments won't last forever.

If our identity begins in how God created us, then all our longings and desires point us back to how things were meant to be. When we search to "find who we are" or "be happy," we are attempting to get back to a place we all know existed and hope can exist again. This is why even the most beautiful moments in our lives are not enough to satisfy.

Some of us, if we are honest, are angry about that. We think such moments *should* last forever. The wise writer of Ecclesiastes said that we have eternity written on our hearts.[16] It's in these moments that we are most aware of that. When we feel such longing, we're embodying a truth of Scripture: we are made for another world. With our very emotions and feelings—with the very firing of synapses in our brains and with the very secretion of chemicals in our neural pathways— we are testifying to the truth of Scripture.

One of my best friends recently lost his baby girl to cancer. There were moments I spent with her that were magical. Moments I wanted to last forever. I can't fathom how many more such moments her mommy and daddy experienced. But those moments didn't last. She's not *here* anymore.

We hate hearing stories like that. We don't accept things like that. No one honestly says, "Well, that's life." That's not life. That's death. That's stupid. That's cancer. That's *not* life.

Why do we experience moments that we wish could last for- ever? Why do we mourn when they don't? Why do we feel like we were built for eternity?

My friend's heart is absolutely broken. Destroyed. He watched cancer hurt and then kill his baby girl. And yet my friend tells me he's already anticipating the joy that will remake his heart one day—the same joy that has already remade his daughter.

"Our Father refreshes us on the journey with some pleasant inns," wrote C. S. Lewis.[17] Just as what we long for often produces pain and a feeling of incompleteness, so also what we long for can lead us to real but temporary happiness. We long for love, and we get married. We long for purpose, and we find a satisfying job. We long for meaning, and we become part of a wonderful church body.

Are these things enough? The rest of Lewis's thought is essential: "But [He] will not encourage us to mistake them for home." No matter how loved or satisfied we feel in this life, it is not satisfaction or love that can last forever. It cannot become our all. It *will* disappoint us ... because it was designed to disappoint us. Or rather, designed to *point* us to something beyond this world.

How can the joy beyond the walls of the world seem so familiar? Because we remember. We have a collective memory of the garden. Of perfection. We all remember, deep down, because it's built into our identity, the *imago Dei*, a memory of who we were created to be, of how life was created to be lived.

A recent book by a neurosurgeon who claims he died and experienced heaven describes it as "when your parents take you back to a place where you spent some time as a very young child. You don't know the place. Or at least you think you don't. But as you look around, something pulls at you, and you realize that a part of yourself—a part way, deep down—does remember the place after all, and is rejoicing at being back there again."[18]

Deep inside our DNA is the memory of a garden. It was a place—the only place—where we humans have ever under-stood our identity fully, a place where what we were *made* to do and what we actually *did* were one and the same. That per-fect place is gone. One day we will return to it, but that day has not yet come. In our best moments, we know this is the place toward which we are living, the place we are designed for.

What does this mean for your identity?

You were created to be something. You were created to live into an identity that the best moments in life can only point to.

In moments when we're tired and lonely and filled with doubt, our certain hope can crumble. The pain can seem to over-whelm the joy. The weight of life can seem too much to bear.

But take heart. For the "joy beyond the walls of the world, poignant as grief" is real. You have been created, designed, to taste that joy now, just as you have been asked to share that joy with others. And one day you will enter that joy, fully, and you will never leave it.

AN END, A BEGINNING

Let's review. We were created in God's image, and perfectly at that. It's why we are all searching for the same things, and it's why—in this life—the deepest joys cannot fully satisfy. We were created *in* this world, but we were created *for* another world.

We were created in a perfect garden and given the chance to live in our true identities. And then we failed.

We fail.

What happened? Why, ever since, have we lived out of identities that aren't the truest things about us?

What we need is a new example. We need to know how to discover and live the truest thing about us *while* living east of Eden, outside the garden. Besides the garden, there is another perfect picture of what it means to be made in the image of God.

It's Jesus. Some people say He's the answer, and while that makes a problematic bumper sticker, in this case I agree.

How can we recover our *imago Dei* and live our true identities?

By meeting Jesus. He is "the image of the invisible God."[19] If you see Him, you have seen the Father.[20] He is "the radiance of God's glory and the exact representation of his being."[21]

And Jesus is the only true human. It's been said that Jesus is what God's love looks like with bones and skin and clothes on. Others have said that Jesus is the theology of God the Father.

Do you want to know what it really, truly, irrevocably means to be made in the image of God and to carry *imago Dei* into the world every day? It means love. Love for God and love for people and love for what God has created. Only one person has ever shown what it looks like for a human to do that perfectly.

He came to show us the way. He came to *make* the way.

THE TRUEST HUMAN
JESUS AND IDENTITY

Define yourself radically as beloved by God. This is
the true self. Every other identity is an illusion.
Brennan Manning, *Abba's Child*

EAST OF EDEN

We long for true happiness. We saw in chapter 3 that the
roots of that reason go deep, reaching all the way back to
the soil of Eden. We were created for Eden, but we live far
from paradise. We know that. That's why we're so familiar
with words like *disappointment, longing, hurt, pain, sin,* and
failure.

The truth is that our longing for good news actually surfaces the bad news; both exist in relationship, and one cannot be understood apart from the other. We long for Eden, but we cannot return to it. In Genesis 3 we read that an angel guards the entrance to the garden with a fiery sword, symbolizing the impossibility of returning to a time before sin, a time when God's shalom was the only show in town.

The title of John Steinbeck's masterpiece sums it up for us: we live *East of Eden*.

If we're going to return to paradise, someone has to lead us. That someone crashed into the middle of human history, and He lived out of a true identity. Not just to show us how, but to take us back.

EXPANSIVE AS THE SKY

One of my wife's favorite quotes is from Corrie ten Boom, who, along with her father, helped many Jews escape the Holocaust during World War II. It goes like this: "If you look at the world, you'll be distressed. If you look within, you'll be depressed. If you look at God, you'll be at rest."

Punchy and very quotable.

It also pertains to our identity. We look *around* to find our identity. We want people to mirror back who we are, but this ends in distress. Or we try to look *within* to find an identity. We follow our desires, our hearts, our wants, and our attractions to know who we are, but we end up depressed.

When we look to God for our identity, however, we can find rest. "God created [humanity]," wrote Bruce Waltke, "and therefore only God can reveal to us our identity and function. Without this biblical revelation, we are lost in a maze of confusion."[1]

Confused.

Distressed.

Depressed.

That about sums it up.

Dale Kuehne created the helpful concept of *iWorld*—a world that is entirely shaped by the individual. The focus here is on the word *I*, from start to finish. Let's look at what it's like to live in such a world:

> The iWorld has a very different conception of identity. In the iWorld, identity is something we are instructed to select or create. If we don't like or aren't comfortable with who we are, *we are encouraged to remake ourselves in*

*whatever manner we are able to and science
will allow.* Consequently, in the iWorld the
search for meaning and self-understanding
can be endless because we are always left to
wonder if we could have been happier if we
had chosen a different path.[2]

That's eerie in its familiarity, at least to me. Encouraged to
remake ourselves in whatever manner we are able? Such
freedom! What more could we ask for, in the post-everything
West, than the autonomy to choose the shape of our own
identities?

But this hasn't helped. We try to "have it both ways" and end
up having it neither way. If I walk into the world's biggest candy
store, I don't just head to the Peanut M&M'S, even though they
are my all-time favorite candy. What if there's something I've
never heard of that I'll like better? What if a different choice
will be more satisfying? So I look and look and look.

This is us. Identity choices as expansive as the sky. And we're
all lost in the endless expanse.

Then what's the alternative? Our *imago Dei*.

Let's look at one more great section from *iWorld*. Kuehne says
that if the roots and trunk of human identity are God, then
the branches of human identity—how we live and think and

dream—are our relationships with God and with others. We simply cannot focus on branches and ignore the roots and trunk, the sources of all life and possibility of growth for the branches. This has incredibly important consequences for our identity.

> According to Christianity, we come to have a more complete understanding of our nature and identity by first developing a love relationship with God, through his son, Jesus. Indeed, the relationship of primary importance for accurately comprehending who we are is our relationship with God. Misunderstanding of our true nature leads to misconception concerning our identity.[3]

Discovering our true identity is about far more than keeping our eyes—and options—open. It matters what we are looking at. It matters who we're looking at.

So let's spend some time getting inside two stories from the life of Jesus, the truest human and the One who has the power to profoundly transform our understanding of identity.

A STRANGE BEGINNING

On a true/false test, many of us would be able to mark a nice capital *T* by the sentence "Jesus was baptized." But let's speed past the fact that it merely happened and instead begin to think together about the strangeness of that event. Some of us know the story well, but if we take a few minutes to hear it with fresh ears, it may sound ... *bizarre*. And if we're going to make sense of what it has to do with identity, that's the way we need to hear it.

We're at the Jordan River, among a large crowd of people. Standing with a clear view of the river—and keeping a bit apart from the common folk—are some of the upper class. These men have clean, elaborate outfits that stand out in such an out-of-the-way place. Then, closer to the water, everyone else is milling about, buzzing with excitement for the newest prophet.

He's the one thing that links all of us together, the guy wearing camel-hair clothes and raving like a lunatic. He's called the Baptizer, and he's brought *all* of us here, for one reason or another.

It's after the usual warnings that things start to change. John starts talking about One who is coming after him, One who will be so powerful and important that John wouldn't even feel worthy lugging around His shoes. Then John says this person will baptize differently as well—that instead of water He'll put people under the burning holiness of God's Spirit.

Suddenly, in a heartbeat, John goes from frantic gesticulating and yelling to silent stillness. He stares into the crowd just as a common man steps out of it. Something changes in John's face. Nothing about the man sets Him apart from the others, except perhaps the way John looks at Him. He's different. He walks directly to the edge of the river, steps into the water, and asks John to baptize Him.

John knows very well who just stepped to the river. It's Jesus, the carpenter's son from Nazareth.

Jesus is the fulfillment of everything John's been working toward. Every time he talked about the One who would follow him, he was waiting for Jesus. Every time he painted a picture of the coming kingdom, he was looking forward to Jesus. And now that Jesus is actually here, standing in the same water, John stops in his tracks. The man who at all other times is so certain, so solid, seems at a loss.

After a long moment during which the two men do nothing but stare at each other, at last John finds his voice.

"I need to be baptized by You—and You're asking *me*?"[4]

Jesus doesn't miss a beat. "Let it be so now; it is proper for us to do this to fulfill all righteousness."[5]

John nods. He grabs the back of Jesus' head with one hand, pushes His chest with the other, and shoves Him under the water. A moment later, Jesus sputters back into the light, finding His footing and wiping water from His face and beard.

Then all of us standing there at the river hear God the Father speak. But more importantly, Jesus hears the Father speak. It's strange—we've never heard anything like that voice, yet it's instantly familiar. And God says, "This is My Son. I love Him, and the fact that He's alive makes me unbearably happy."[6]

Jesus is standing there, dripping water, positively glowing from the grace of those divine words, and all of us realize that those words are what we've been waiting to hear our whole lives.

ONE OF US

We know Jesus was baptized, and we know John was reluctant to baptize Him, but one thing we may not have thought about is *why* Jesus had to be baptized. He clearly didn't *need* to be baptized for the same reasons as everyone else who ventured to the Jordan River—to repent of sin and symbolize the beginning of a new life following God's commands. But there was still a sense in which He *needed* to be baptized. John didn't want to do it, but Jesus insisted.

If you're having trouble picturing the role reversal that happened there, imagine a surgeon stepping to the side of the operating table, handing the scalpel to the patient, and asking, "Will you operate on me?" When we think of it this way, the absurdity of the scene stands out in sharp relief. The one who should have been repenting, John, was baptizing the only perfect person present, Jesus.

Since Jesus was an "exact representation" of God,[7] He could certainly do whatever He wanted. But the God of the Bible is not a capricious deity who changes His mind and plans just for the heck of it. In fact, the God of the Bible is the opposite: "the same yesterday and today and forever,"[8] the One who chose His children "before the foundation of the world."[9]

No, Jesus' baptism was planned for a specific reason, and it took place in a specific way. I believe one reason is this: Jesus was baptized so that He could identify with you.

It's more familiar to think about Jesus' birth in terms of God becoming human as a means of identification. When Jesus was born to Mary, He took on the limitations of His creations in order to identify with His creations.

We're less familiar, however, with that same thing happening at the Jordan River. That day, when Jesus stepped into the sinners' water beside John the Baptizer, He was stating unequivocally that He was identifying Himself with us. Although He was sinless, He would go beneath the water like a repentant sinner, and like a repentant sinner He would be raised out of the water and into new life. This act, for Jesus, was a two-part symbol, because its significance echoed past the virtual death of baptism and into the literal death of the cross. The movement of the cross is the movement of baptism: displayed for the world to see, descending into the grave, and being raised back up into a new life.

Earlier I said that Jesus was baptized so that He could identify with you, and I want to draw your attention to a particular word in that sentence. *You.*

I know, I know—I've spent a bunch of chapters trying to get us to take the focus off of ourselves, but in this case the navel-gazing is necessary.

There is something absolutely stunning about the fact that the God of the Bible is a God who exists and acts both outside of time and inside human history. Before creating the world, God spent an eternity in perfect love and communion with His triune Self, just as God will exist for eternity future when this world is brought to its intended end. Despite the cosmic scope of God's activity—or perhaps, in a way only God can understand, *because* of it—God is making *you* part of His plan and activity.

Even more unbelievably, God was already making you part of His plan and activity two thousand years before you were conceived! Part of the reason Jesus was baptized was to symbolize what He planned on doing for you: going under the waters of death and rising into the light of new life.

And now, when *we* choose to be baptized, we are saying to Jesus, "You chose to identify with us, so we choose to identify ourselves with You."

THE WORDS JESUS HEARS

If Hollywood was to do Jesus' baptism, it would not be staged at that point in His biography. The words from heaven that identified Jesus would not be spoken until later. Much later. *After* His ministry. *After* He healed multitudes. *After* temptation was fought and conquered. *After* the cross. *After* He *did* something! At the point in His life that Jesus was baptized, He hadn't *done* anything.

Scripture mentions Jesus only once between the time He was an infant and the time He entered public ministry at age thirty. The single story happened when He was twelve and traveling to Jerusalem with His family. While in the city, Jesus headed to the temple and began to talk with the religious leaders—and it wasn't until three days later that His parents finally noticed Jesus was missing and tracked Him down.

But that's it. As far as we know, Jesus hadn't *done* anything. We can assume that He lived as a carpenter, taking His father's trade, because that's what people did back then. He didn't marry, which was very unusual in that culture. And then at age thirty, He showed up at the Jordan River and heard His Father in heaven declare that Jesus pleases Him!

Why? Because He was a good carpenter? Because He obeyed His parents? Because He wanted to learn more about God?

No. Having done nothing we would think worthy of praise, Jesus heard God's declaration about His identity. *Before* He completed the work He was given to do, Jesus heard what was truest about Him.

And what telling words they were—words that echo back in time before the world was created and into the perfect joy of God's eternity: *"This is my Son, whom I love; with him I am well pleased."*[10]

Think about that for a minute. Let it soak in.

Here is a scene where a father is telling his son something that is intimate and wonderful. These moments don't happen often enough in our world.

Henri Nouwen pointed out that we find an identity in part through what others say about us. What others say about us can shape our self-identity in profound ways. Identities are not found; they are given. For many of us, identities are given by people who don't have the right to identify us.

True identities can be given only by God.

Jesus' identity was given to Him by His heavenly Father—*and before He did anything to "earn" approval*, He was shaped by God's declaration.

You are My Son.

I love You.

I'm pleased with You.

Jesus made the Father proud because of the simple fact of who He was.

A recent book I read opens with a piercing question: "Imagine God thinking about you. What do you assume God feels when you come to mind?"[11] The author wrote that a large number of people say they imagine God feels disappointment.

What if the words Jesus heard after coming out of the water that day were, "You are My Son, and I'm only provisionally pleased with You. Don't disappoint Me. You better not screw this up. Have a good life"?

Instead, Jesus was given an identity by His Father, and the identity was one of love. The beloved. Jesus received that identity and then lived in it, as if it was the truest thing about Him. Because it was.

Today we wonder, "What about *my* identity? Do I have any hope of living like Jesus did? Can what Jesus learned about identity help me?"

I believe the answer to those questions is *yes*, but in order to see that, we need to tell another story about something that happened directly after Jesus was baptized. Jesus, fresh from hearing what the God of the universe thought about Him, was sent into a time of intense testing and trials. It took place in a literal wilderness, full of danger, and the outcome of the test defined the shape of Jesus' life and changed the course of human history.

We cannot enter our own wilderness of life, our own time of testing, unless we follow the arc of Jesus' life—unless our hair is still wet with baptism identity.[12]

TEMPTED LIKE US

After Jesus was baptized He spent some time alone. A *lot* of time—almost six weeks, according to Matthew. We Christians like to talk about quiet times and solitude and shutting off the distractions of the world, but we're hard-pressed to pull off forty *minutes* of that. When was the last time you were in a place of total silence? No buzz of random conversation around you in the coffee shop, no music on your headphones, no checking your smartphone—just you and total silence.

Even when we are alone, in silence, what noises run through our heads? Conversations, to-do lists, or worst of all, commercial jingles from the '80s. (Now you know what my brain looks like.) If we ever do manage complete silence, we sometimes see the arrival of temptation, perhaps because we begin to think about all the junk hiding inside us that we didn't notice because of our constant busyness.

Jesus knew this temptation. When God's Spirit led Him into the desert, Jesus had no resources. No baggage. No gear. He simply walked into the desert, found some water and probably a cave or an overhang, and proceeded to wait.

Having just been identified at the Jordan River by His Father's voice from heaven, Jesus was about to find out what that identity *meant*. And this discovery would take place during an unimaginably difficult time of isolation, fear, and temptation. In the Judean desert Jesus would face profound testing. He would be completely isolated. He would be broken down by hunger and loneliness. He would be scared by wild animals and surrounded by echoing silence.

This entire desert trial happened in God's timing and plan. God understood all along that His Son, before beginning three years of intensely public preaching and healing and confrontation, needed to be tempted. Or perhaps *tempered* is a better word, a word that means making a material both stronger *and* more flexible. Doesn't that describe Jesus—a counterintuitive paradox of ultimate strength and humble flexibility?

After Jesus waited alone and in silence for forty days, Satan showed up. Since this is the first time we've talked about him in this book, I want to take a very short detour. There is a lot of misinformation floating around about Satan. Some doubt he is real, while others obsess about him. Both of these errors were highlighted by C. S. Lewis in *The Screwtape Letters*. Lewis reminded us that Satan is quite happy with either mistake—ignorance or obsession—because both let him work his subtle and insidious plans.

Now, Satan *is* real, so don't ignore him, but he is not God's equal foe. Satan is limited in his temporal power, and he has already been conquered in the eternal scheme of history by the death and resurrection of Jesus, so obsessing about him serves no purpose. The point here is that, according to orthodox Christian theology, we can say several things about Satan. He is a real being, he has supernatural powers, he works to cause evil in the world, and he is not God's equal counterpart. This is the understanding of Satan upon which I'm operating in this book, and I'm not going to take any more time speculating beyond that.

We need to keep reminding ourselves that Jesus really *was* tempted throughout His life. We shouldn't picture Jesus kind of floating through life, detached from what was happening around Him. *What's that? I'm being tempted? Ho hum ... water off a duck's back.* Staying sinless is a lot easier if it's impossible to sin. So there was something in Satan's offer that was a serious temptation to Jesus. There was a real chance that one of the things Satan offered would be what caused Jesus to claim a new, self-defined identity.

What did it really mean, after all, to be "beloved of God"? And what if there was something better?

Satan asked Jesus three questions. Since He was so hungry, why didn't He make Himself bread? If He was really the Son of God, why didn't He leap from the top of the temple and let the angels save Him? And if He wanted to save people all over the world, why didn't He worship Satan and receive all the kingdoms of the world? The ways He was tempted were very human. *Eat and drink whatever you want. Prove yourself. If you had more power, you could do more good. Get everything you want to complete what God has given you to do. You can have it, right here and right now.*

These things still tempt us today.

FALSE IDENTITIES

Satan tempted Jesus to live out of a false sense of self. He used the continued phrase, "If you really are the Son of God ..."

Jesus had just heard God's voice over Him, and now He was hearing the competing voice of Satan. Satan tends to tempt us with similar questions. *Is that who you really are? What if you were someone else?*

Part of Jesus wanted to receive affirmation by flexing His own miracle-muscles to make bread, by calling down angels from heaven to save Him, or by taking possession of every kingdom on earth. Don't forget that Scripture calls it temptation for a reason.

So why didn't Satan's plan work? Because Jesus knew His identity given to Him by the Father. *I know who I am because before the Spirit sent Me to be tempted, My Father spoke for all to hear: I am the beloved of God.*

Jesus was tempted to live out of false identities. He chose to live out of the truest thing instead.

The next time you are tempted to live out of false identities, what will you choose?

In His very bones Jesus knew that He was God's beloved Son, that He made God happy just by existing. That was a truth, a lesson, that was impossible to forget. Not only had Jesus just experienced it at the Jordan River in a public, profound way, but He'd been experiencing the truth of it throughout His life. Compared to that level of ultimate truth, Satan's offers could never appear more than counterfeit. Sometimes a counterfeit can deceive, but only when we don't have the genuine article to compare it to.

Jesus was able to own His identity in trust and confidence and live out of the fact that He was beloved by God. Jesus' hair was still wet with His baptism identity, and in every temptation, He chose to live out of the truest thing about Himself.

This comes full circle in the gospel of John, just before Jesus is betrayed and killed. After sharing a final meal with His friends, He wraps a servant's towel around Himself and fills a bowl with water. Then He kneels at the feet of His disciples, one by one, and washes their feet—"handles their very toes."[13]

This was the King of the universe, washing road dirt from underneath toenails. Where did He get that impulse? John revealed the answer when he wrote that Jesus, *knowing where He came from and where He was going*, chose to wash their feet.[14]

That's identity. The deep knowledge of where I come from, where I'm going, and to whom I belong.

Jesus fully understood His identity from the moment His Father spoke it over Him. And that confidence in His identity allowed Him to live His entire life of ministry and ultimately fulfill what God had given Him to do.

Discovering our true identity, then, makes us capable of things that would otherwise destroy us.

Did you consider, when you opened this book, that learning the truest thing about yourself might have the power to lead you into the desert? That finding your identity might unmake you?

I confess that I didn't when I started writing it.

ME, PART TWO

My identity crisis wasn't glamorous. Well, my wilderness test did happen in a small beach town on the California coast, so in that sense it was a bit glamorous. That part was nothing like forty days in the wilderness.

After I was fired from the bank, I worked at a Starbucks and as a security guard at the local high school. Some of the kids called me "young blood" like we were in an old Western and I was the new deputy who was too young for his own good.

My circumstances were different, but the nature of my testing was the same: "What is the truest thing about me?"

If I was asked that question I would have answered, "I'm beloved of God."

But those would have just been words. After living a year in obscurity, after being fired from counting money, after putting on the green apron every morning at 4:30 a.m., and, after carrying a walkie-talkie and telling kids to get to class on time in the afternoon, I realized I really believed that the truest thing about me was *I was my career.*

It's humiliating to admit, but it was true. I wasn't anyone unless I was moving forward in my career, and I was stuck in the slowest holding pattern ever.

And then came the point when it seemed my career would be kick-started again. The call came. I would be sent to San Francisco to start a church. But I wasn't qualified to start a church in a city like that! Since my identity was wrapped up in my career, and the taste of being fired was still fresh in my mouth, I knew San Francisco would be an epic fail.

This spun me into depression. I "went dark." That was the phrase coined by my friends after they'd been attempting to get in touch with me for days. My wife tried to encourage me. Prayed for me. Told my friends on me. She called them and said that I wasn't doing well and they needed to intervene.

I didn't want an intervention though—I just wanted my old life back.

The life without much risk. The one where I was secure in my career and my public identity. I didn't even know who I was anymore. I thought I was secure in God's love for me, but after months of "wilderness" temptation, all that pretense fell off. It became clear that my identity was built on something else. Something that I would never have known or admitted.

I'm not going to pretty up this story and pretend that I had a single moment when heaven parted and God the Father spoke my identity over me. I wish that had happened. It didn't. Discovering the truest thing about myself was a process. God had to confirm to me over and over again:

"You are not what you do."

"You are not what you have."

"You are not what you desire."

Over and over again.

It took several trips to San Francisco, all spent praying. It took many late-night conversations with God. It took me playing what-if with every possible worst-case scenario.

And slowly it clicked. If I went to San Francisco and utterly failed, it wouldn't change anything. I was beloved of God. Even if I earned a reputation. "Oh yeah, Dave, he tried, he failed, now he's back in Bakersfield, working at Trader Joe's." So what? That wouldn't change a thing. (And who knows—it might still happen!)

Slowly, achingly slowly, I was learning to understand that I am deeply loved by God, and because of Jesus, God is well pleased with *me*.

Every other identity I create for myself is an illusion.

QUESTIONS AND ANSWERS

Isn't it pointless or even dangerous to use Jesus as an example? He was perfect. He was the Son of God. What chance do we have? If we're going to look to Jesus to discover how to withstand the temptation of embracing false identities, we may as well use Him as a case study for how to rise from the dead!

Jesus was tempted and passed—but that isn't fair.

I would definitely have jumped off the temple. I mean, that sounds really fun. You only live once (YOLO!), and here I'm being given a chance to do something epic, something I can tell people about at parties. I'll be famous. I'll trend on Twitter. People will whisper as I walk into the room, "Hey, there's that guy who jumped off the pinnacle of the temple and lived to tell about it!"

In other words, I would have failed. A thousand ways and a million times.

So we can't really use Jesus as an example, right? In this case I say we *can*.

Remember *why* Jesus told John that He had to be baptized. Jesus could have acquiesced to John's protest; when John said that he shouldn't be baptizing Jesus, Jesus could have agreed. Jesus could have been like, "You're right, John! Everyone in the world needs to be baptized ... except for Me. I'm good. Move on down the line."

But that isn't what happened. Jesus was baptized because He wanted to step into our mess. He *wanted* to. Jesus didn't become human because He got stuck with it, as if Plans A, B, and C didn't work out and He ran out of options.

No—Jesus *wanted* to become human, to enter our world, for a simple reason. He wanted to because He wanted *us*.

He did it to *identify* with us.

He did it to identify with *us*.

His own identity never changed. What His Father declared at the Jordan River—"This is My beloved Son, in whom I am well pleased"[15]—was true before the world was created, and it will remain true throughout eternity. Jesus was God's beloved. But in becoming human, Jesus both identified with humanity and declared to humanity our true identity.

Here's the good news of all good news: our identity is the same as Jesus'!

Beloved.

Child of God.

In whom God is well pleased.

Don't believe me? Too good to be true?

Jesus became human to take on the powers that try to make us into what we are not.

Jesus became human to go under:

under the limitations of flesh and bone

under the waters of baptism

under the wrath of God

... and ultimately under the curse of death.

Jesus was baptized to identify with us. And now we are baptized to identify with Him. If you go to a liturgical church, you'll be familiar with the poetic repetition of "Christ has died, Christ has risen, Christ will come again" that is part of the Eucharist. Baptism identifies us with Jesus. It puts words in our mouths—words built on the foundation of Jesus' perfect life.

The baptism of Jesus pointed forward. Forward about three years to when Jesus would step into our place in the most profound and powerful way. The choice Jesus made to identify with us didn't stop at birth, baptism, or even the wilderness. That choice carried Him all the way to death on a Roman cross. On the cross He identified with us for this reason: it was our sin He carried on that cross.

It might be that you've never heard God say to you, "You are My beloved." And yes, perhaps when you imagine God thinking about you, all that comes to your mind is disappointment.

Or cold silence.

When Jesus was roped and nailed to that cross, somehow He experienced and carried our sin and our failures. Shame and rejection stung Him. And what did He hear from His Father then?

Nothing.

The cruelest kind of silence.

That's when Jesus cried out, "My God, my God, why have you forsaken me?"[16] I read once that we could start that quote at the question mark and still clearly see Jesus' identification with us.[17]

As Frederick Dale Bruner noted, Jesus *could* have ended His life much more triumphantly than with a question. He could have left His followers, and posterity, with a noble exclamation. Perhaps "God is love!" or even "I'll be back—see you in three days!"

Instead, Jesus died asking questions. Does that sound familiar? He "not only took on our flesh and blood but also our nervous systems."[18] He took on our brains and hearts and gut feelings.

Yes, He absolutely came to give us answers.[19] But He also came to ask our questions. Like, why is God sometimes silent? Like, why can it feel like we're forsaken on this planet?

We deserve to be forsaken as Jesus was, but instead we receive affirmation and love. We deserve the silence that surrounded Jesus, but instead He gives us the words of eternal life.

Hebrews 12:2 says that Jesus ran the race of life for a reason: the joy set before Him. That's a strange statement. Didn't

Jesus already have every possible joy before time existed, before there was even an earth? Not quite. There was one joy He had to become human to get. You. Me. All of us who call on Him. If life was a race Jesus ran, saving us was the prize. And the race cost Jesus everything, including His own life as He slowly suffocated on a crude cross.

Jesus *chose* to do that. And because of what Jesus did, the words He heard at His baptism become yours. The identity that shaped His life now shapes yours.

As you give up every effort to save yourself, you can be saved. You must stop trying to save yourself and begin to cling to the only One who can save you.

In Christ, you are the beloved of God.

5

OUR HUMAN CONDITION
THE SKIN WE LIVE IN

And I thought to myself, oh dear, however
many skins have I got to take off?

Eustace, *The Voyage of the Dawn Treader*

DRAGONED

In C. S. Lewis's *The Voyage of the Dawn Treader*, we meet an
English schoolboy named Eustace who has, against his will,
been taken into a magical country called Narnia. It is a country
replete with talking animals and chivalrous swordplay, with sea
serpents and adventures waiting to be had. He considers it a
beastly place, but we soon learn it is really the boy who is beastly.

Eustace's identity as a self-absorbed twit colors the way he sees everything: where he is, who he's with, the choices he makes.

The ship *The Dawn Treader*, captained by King Caspian, is sailing east into the unknown. In the sixth chapter of the story, while his shipmates reprovision on an island, Eustace wanders away. Lost in the hills, Eustace shelters from a downpour in a cave. It is the cave of a dragon, and Eustace, "sleeping on a dragon's hoard with greedy, dragonish thoughts in his heart," transforms into a dragon.[1]

This isn't some fairy tale for children only.

It is the story of how we become who we hate, how the worst parts of us manage to find the light. Have you ever looked in the mirror and thought, *How did I become this?*

How did I let that eating disorder overtake every part of my life?

How did I let that bad relationship ruin every relationship thereafter?

How did I let that loss keep me from trusting anyone again?

How did I let failure define every decision I currently make?

We become the identities we hate. We hate the identities we become. We're not talking about some story here. We become, like Eustace, dragoned.

When did you last feel the weight of becoming a dragon? Was it when you looked around the lunchroom of your latest job, hating the small talk and the smell of your reheated pasta? Or when you woke alone, tangled in the wrinkled sheets of a stranger's bed?

We wake, if we wake at all, as a dragon, and life is never the same.

SKIN DEEP

For Eustace, waking as a dragon becomes a moment of epiphany. All along he's been made for something else—something more noble—but he cannot realize this until the option is taken from him.

As a dragon, then, what once he shunned becomes what he wants. Human friendship, purpose, hard work done well and with a willing spirit—these that he once hated become what dragon-Eustace pursues.

To these new ends, he hunts goats for his former shipmates and invites them to curl against his warm, scaled body during the coldest part of the night. In pantomime he seeks conversation. He becomes an amusement-park ride, giving aerial tours to the bravest adventurers. He tries, in short, to be the best dragon he can be, and that, it turns out, is a significant improvement on the boy he was. He tries to change himself, and it works out better than he could have hoped.

Here's the easy moral: it's never too late to make a new start and live a better life.

Eustace might have been a dragon, and he might have regretted the years wasted on living for nothing beyond his stomach and his narrow mind, but he's given a second chance to reinvent himself. A new identity can atone for the sins of an old identity, and it's up to Eustace to fix things, to save himself, to try to make things right.

We try to do the same. Less time with those friends and more time with these. Yoga. A new wardrobe for a new job. Or, as one musician quipped, "I'm a new man / I wear a new cologne."[2] We try being more patient, more driven, more of everything that will make life better. We might even try a new church.

We can't go back in time and fix the past—those mistakes will follow us—but we always have a choice to reinvent ourselves in the present in order to make things right. Right?

We see the problem, of course. We see all the messiness leaking from that easy moral, staining this page with what-ifs and regrets.

Here's the obvious truth. Reinventing ourselves doesn't work. I mean, it may work for a season. Losing a hundred pounds *will* change things. Dating the "perfect person" might go a long way to medicate that loneliness. But we become neurotic. We have to *keep off the weight*; we have to *keep the person we love*. We've just traded identities. We had one; now we have another. Our new identity may be more noble, more socially accepted, more what we might call "us"—but we can't disguise the fact that we're piling new selves on top of old ones.

Yet we continue to tell ourselves a story that says everything is going to work out as soon as we make *one* more change to our identity.

And one more after that.

It's a story that lets us get out of bed in the morning—but only in fleeting moments of honesty do we admit to ourselves it isn't actually true. And all the while, identities keep adding up.

Piling on ...

like scales.

And then, one day without warning, the mirror again holds a dragon.

SCALES

Amid the static of our competing identities, we can't forget about a beastly boy who becomes a literal beast—and then longs to change back into who he truly is. In the story of Narnia, what is the truest thing about Eustace? It is this two-part truth: he is scaled and no longer wants to be, yet he cannot remove his scales.

You are a dragon. I know because I am one as well.

Being dragoned is the human condition. It is the state of your friends, your family, your coworkers, and the people you pass in the street. Each of us is scaled, just as each of us is skilled at adding to our serpentine armor.

One more week of evening overtime. One more week-end of being tethered to your devices. What's one more layer of scales? This is just a busy season for you at work, and it's worth it. Things will get easier once you land that account, earn that promotion, gain that respect. You'll have time for the rest of your life later, but right now it's all about the job. It's not easy, but you know it's the right decision. It's the same line you heard your father say when you were a kid, inviting him to your baseball game. At the time you knew it was a lie, knew you didn't matter to him, but now that you're older you see it for what it is: the way life works.

Sometimes it's hard to feel through all the scaly layers, but this time it will be different. He won't treat you like your last boyfriend did, or the ten before that. You can tell. There's something special about him. You've watched your friends burning through relationships like matchsticks, bright and vivid and gone in a flash. That's not what you want. It's why you keep dating, keep looking, keep giving your heart away—because you know that the right one is out there, waiting. Maybe this time your heart won't break. Maybe this time you won't hole up in your apartment for days, alone with your wine rack and a sink full of dishes. It isn't easy, but if that's what it takes to find love and happiness, you're willing to play the game.

Why do we add scales? To survive. Because we must. Our scales shift, changing colors and thickness, but scaled we remain. Layers of identity accrete, slowly thickening from the moment the lightbulb of self-consciousness is lit. How many layers can you feel when you shift in your seat? When you grip the steering wheel?

You layer fresh scales on yourself with every new identity you add. The iterations you've gone through to protect yourself, to find yourself, to remake yourself are countless. How long did it take for overachiever to cover brokenhearted? For activist to cover consumer?

Can you remember one time in your life when you've touched something without touching it through scales?

SELF-SURGERY

Later in *The Voyage of the Dawn Treader*, Eustace huddles away from the warmth of his friends, alone with his thoughts. It is dark, and darkness amplifies the pain, it amplifies the loneliness. Alone in the dark, reality becomes just a little too real.

When the longing to become human again overtakes Eustace, he sinks his claws into himself. He pulls, he peels, and off sloughs his old identity like snakeskin. He is a new creature, but only for the time it takes him to walk to the water to be washed. There he sees himself, and nothing has changed. Beneath his dragon scales he remains a dragon, and though he repeats the self-surgery, the prognosis is the same.

Have you taken your cue from Eustace and tried to be the best dragon you can be? After all, what's the alternative?

You don and shed identities without knowing who you are at the core—if there is even a core to know. With no essential you, all that remains is to be the best you can be at any given moment. Have you tried to remove identities you no longer want by hard work or willpower or neglect?

Do you believe the only answer is self-surgery?

Eustace discovers the trouble soon enough.

> And I thought to myself, oh dear, however
> many skins have I got to take off?[3]

How many skins have you got to take off? The answer is as simple as it is impossible. Always one more.

....

As Eustace tries to strip away his false identity, he is watched by a lion called Aslan—the messiah figure in the story. Aslan is described by another creature in Narnia as never safe but always good.[4] Eustace looks up from his latest attempt to transform himself to find Aslan watching. Waiting. And then speaking. "You will have to let me undress you."[5]

The truest thing about Eustace has been hidden, even from his own heart.

Especially from his own heart.

Don't we remain strangers to ourselves? Don't we wander, in Walker Percy's phrase, "lost in the cosmos," desperate to be known and named by other people while such definition continues to escape us? Scales added, scales ripped off—and all the while we feel we are watched.

If identity is fluid, then to remain still is to die—or worse, to become irrelevant—and so we never cease our frantic movement in the direction we hope, and pray, is forward. New job. No job. That man, that woman, making casual what is sacred or elevating to the status of a god a broken idol.

And yet the impossibility remains. We cannot undress ourselves, just as we cannot fully know the self we long to undress. The only One who can undress us, who can remove the lifetime of layers, who knows the truest thing, and everything, about us, is the One who created us. All our lives He has been watching. Read the poem of a scrawny shepherd to see how early it begins or the letter of a tentmaker to see how far it extends.[6]

Our watcher has been waiting for the moment we sheath our *own* claws in order to reveal *His*.

Dragon-Eustace throws up his hands in despair. But it is despair mixed with hope. If ever it can be different, it will be this time.

We try in vain to tear our own scales off. We try in vain to inhabit new identities. As Eustace at last understands, we cannot change ourselves, just as we cannot save ourselves.

Aslan unfolds his claws, and the dragon holds still.

"The first tear he made was so deep," recalls Eustace, "that I thought it had gone right into my heart. When he began pulling the skin off, it hurt worse than anything I've ever felt. The only thing that made me able to bear it was the pleasure of seeing the stuff peel off."[7]

UNDRAGONED

Uncovering the truest thing about you isn't a project. It isn't self-help. It isn't something to journal about on your day off or discuss with your friends.

The truest thing about you isn't how you act or how you want to start acting. It isn't the ways you've acted in the past or the pain that has been acted upon you. It isn't how you feel or how you wish you felt.

The truest thing about you isn't the names you've given yourself or the names that have been given to you.

Dragon-Eustace, as he lies helpless on his back, discovers that the truest thing about him is a question answered only by the pierce and pull of claws.

The claws that can cut to your heart are the claws that can heal.

Eustace looks up, his breath ragged, and he learns the secret of identity. "There it was lying on the grass: only ever so much thicker, and darker, and more knobbly-looking than the [other skins] had been."[8]

Beneath your scales waits a naked boy, a naked girl, more beautiful and beloved than you can imagine.

Do you long to take off everything that isn't you? Do you long to shed at last the weight of false identity?

Face the claws, breathe deep, and ask.

This is truth, and it is the truest thing about you: if you have come with your scales and scars to Jesus, to the Lion of Judah, then you have been undragoned.

"No. It wasn't a dream."

"Why not?"

"You have been—well, un-dragoned ..."[9]

6

OUR GREATEST HOPE
THE TRUEST THING ABOUT YOU

*From the moment we claim the truth of being the Beloved,
we are faced with the call to become who we are.*

Henri Nouwen, *Spiritual Direction*

REIMAGINE

Being undragoned means being given a new identity. A complete transformation. Living a new identity means going through a metamorphosis as radical as one from a dragon into a boy.

The basis of our new identity in Jesus is love—God's love and the love demonstrated by Jesus' life, death, and resurrection.

The result of our new identity is a new, reimagined under-standing of our relationship with all of life. We reimagine what it means to be human. We reimagine what it means to be male or female, rich or poor, powerful or powerless. We reimagine what it means to be sexual or celibate, gay or straight, married or single. Most of the letters in the New Testament confront this very thing, helping new followers of Jesus reimagine life as they know it.

What we rarely remember, however—or what we need to learn—is that such a transformation will be frightening. That it might involve a call to die.

FEAR AND TREMBLING

You may know the story: Blondin, the great tightrope master, asks his admirers at Niagara Falls if they believe he can carry someone on his back across the river.

He is answered with a roared chorus of *yeses* and *of courses.*

But when he asks for a volunteer, the crowd falls silent. No one is willing to climb on Blondin's back. None of the people are willing to do what their words plainly meant. Everyone is willing to pretend belief.

That's the part of the story you may know. It is the part of the story told most often because it illustrates a simple point: what we say doesn't always match the way we act. That is true, and it is a lesson worth remembering. But right now we are after something more elusive, and it is to the slippery part of the story we turn.

Blondin knows he can carry a person on his back as he crosses the tightrope above Niagara Falls. He can feel the certainty in his bones just as he can feel the constant thrumming voice of many waters.

No one will climb on Blondin's back, however, so the task falls to his manager. Perhaps he's something of a daredevil himself, or more likely he's thinking of the sales and marketing possibilities. He knows the stuff he is made of—this is a thing he can do, though he may need help beyond himself. He walks quickly into the nearby hotel, orders a scotch at the bar, neat, and tosses it back. He then opens the door, and the sound of what he is about to do washes over him.

Minutes later, he finds himself clinging to Blondin's back, holding on for his literal life fifteen stories above the roiling surface of the Niagara River. He looks down and sees a wire the width of his wrist. And then he and Blondin almost die.

Feeling a subtle shift in balance, the manager is compelled to lean his weight to the other side. It's a natural response. Though this is a stunt for Blondin, for the manager it is the closest he has ever come to death. He can see the end of his days pouring over and over below him, water thrashing into spray that reaches him and Blondin even on their wired perch. He can hear mortality roaring in his ears; he can taste mortality in the back of his throat.

Wind again, another shift in balance. He is about to die, so he tries to save himself.

Blondin's feet freeze. Above the sound of the water the manager hears Blondin screaming. Every word is an exclamation point. *Stop. Only cling to me. If you want to live, do nothing but cling to me.*

The manager listens because he knows Blondin is right. He adjusts the grip of his hands, recommits the muscles of his arms and legs to encircling Blondin's taut body. Then he gives up trying to balance, trying to make a difference, trying to save his own life. He gives up, and holds on, and waits for what comes.

When Blondin steps from the wire and onto the ground on the other side of the Niagara River, he is lifted onto the shoulders of his admirers, while the manager sinks to the ground, now shaking like a leaf.

I have been told this is a true story, and I believe it is. Yet it scarcely matters. If Niagara Falls were a myth and Blondin and his manager figments of my imagination, this story would remain true, because it is the story of God, and of us, and of what it means to follow the Son of God. I taste the truth of this story because it is the story of my life.

You cannot save yourself.

There is nothing you can do to contribute to your own survival in any ultimate sense. You can add a year here, a decade there, a season of happiness and fulfillment between spring and fall. But you cannot save yourself. When you try to save yourself you will fail. Only when you want to live so badly that you give up trying to save your own life—only then do you have any chance. It is only when you do nothing but cling that you will find yourself carried to safety.

This is a hard truth. It is hard enough to accept when we are crossing a waterfall on a tightrope, never mind when we are crossing the distance between birth and death, the distance between what always was and what will be for-ever. But truth remains—and hope, too.

It is only when the old has passed that the new will come.

LOOK TO CHRIST

Jesus calls us to die.

> Whoever wants to be my disciple must deny
> themselves and take up their cross and follow

me. For whoever wants to save their life will
lose it, but whoever loses their life for me will
find it.[1]

That's a tough word. It's intense. Jesus says, straight out, that
we have to be willing to die if we want to follow Him.

But why? It's not because being a Christian means that our
selves die and we become subsumed into some greater
whole. It doesn't mean we are no longer individuals. Some
religions teach that, but it isn't what Jesus is getting at.

Jesus calls us to die, but not for the sake of death.

Rather, Jesus calls us to die for the sake of true life. *I want you
to die*, He says, *because that is the only way by which you
can enter into real life*.

Most of the time we live as if the opposite were true. We are
so desperate to live, and so afraid of death, that we hold with
white knuckles anything claiming to give us life and identity.
Careers. Possessions. Relationships. We gather these things
into a barrier around ourselves, hoping to keep ourselves safe.

Jesus deconstructs our desperation.

Jesus knows we long for a true identity, an identity that can
never change or be taken from us. Jesus knows we long to

truly be alive. He knows these things because He created us. And so He calls us to take up our crosses and follow Him, because it is on the road to our deaths that our lives can finally begin.

Whoever wants to save their life ... That's a rhetorical beginning to a sentence if I've ever heard one. We *all* want that. It's the human condition. It's what motivates us to act in sometimes desperate ways. And Jesus speaks the truth to us that the only way to get what we want—to save our lives—is to lose our lives for Him and for the gospel.

To receive our true identity from Jesus, we must first let go of the false identities we hold.

The Greek word for *life* that the gospel writer Mark used is *psyche* (sook-ay), from which we get *psychology*. It means your personhood and personality and identity at the core of your being. Listen again to what Jesus is saying.

For whoever wants to save their identity *will lose it, but whoever loses their* identity *for me and for the gospel will find it.*

What if you gained everything you ever wanted—but in the process lost your identity, your unique individuality? Is that a trade you'd make? Or would you rather save forever the unique, beloved child of God at the heart of your identity? Is that something you'd give up everything else to attain?

Jesus provides us with the conditions for finding our true selves. To save our lives we have to stop trying to save our own lives. We have to die to that idea. To that pursuit. And when we do, we discover that Jesus saves our lives and in the process gives us clear vision. We see who we *really* are for the first time.

"Look for yourself," said C. S. Lewis in *Mere Christianity*, "and you will find in the long run only hatred, loneliness, despair, rage, ruin, and decay. But look to Christ and you will find Him, and with Him everything else thrown in."[2]

THE NEW YOU

Your new identity is a total reimagining of who you are compared to who you were. When you reimagine life by looking to Christ for transformation, you do not become *You 2.0*. You aren't simply given an *improved* life, like being given a better address in a nicer neighborhood in the kingdom of darkness. Jesus transfers you from the kingdom of darkness to the kingdom of light. It's new life. Life completely reimagined.

You are not a little nicer, a little better, or a bit less sinful.

You *might* be those things, of course. A new identity in Christ does not prevent you from being nicer, or better, or less sinful. In fact, following Jesus actually contributes a good deal to the likelihood of those things happening. But that is not what we are talking about here. These small, surface-level improve-ments are not, properly speaking, what a new identity *does*.

No, when we call out to Jesus for rescue, that is exactly what happens—immediately we are rescued. Saved. Snatched from the lions' den. Jesus, God's eternal Word and the One in whom we and all of creation live and move and have our being, is the only One who can stage such a rescue mission.

Jesus reaches down into the river of human sin and sorrow under which we're drowning. Jesus, the One whose hands carry scars of His love for us, pulls us bodily from the water and lifts us into new life.

Not nicer or better or less sinful life.

New life. Life reimagined from top to bottom.

The moment we call out to Him, we find ourselves already saved. Just as there is no earthly or heavenly power that can separate us from His love, so there is no earthly or heavenly power that can delay or prolong the rescue mission by which we are transformed.

The old has gone; the new has come.

The rescue mission does not begin with a list of conditions. Jesus does not ask us to shave and shower first, or to try to show Him that we're getting our act together and are worthy candidates for the kingdom of light.

The rescue mission begins, instead, while we are still a long way off, just as it did for the prodigal son. It begins the moment we turn our hearts toward home, for in that moment we discover that our heavenly Father is already running toward us with good news: we were loved before we were born, and before the creation of the world the mission to rescue us was already under way.

New life is not about earning God's love before we return, but rather looking up to find Him already declaring our new identity and waiting with open arms.

When we're given a new identity, Jesus reorders our whole life. It's a top-to-bottom reimagining. If that's the case, we're in for a serious shake-up—but we can trust the One who is doing the shaking.

NOW, TO MAKE THEM GOOD LITTLE CHRISTIANS ...

New Year's 2010. That's when I was part of a team that started a new church in San Francisco. Leading up to our first Sunday-morning gatherings, twenty-three of us committed our lives to this new venture. On the first Sunday I told my friend Tarik to set up twenty chairs, but he insisted on fifty. Triple that showed up. The next month we'd doubled that. By the beginning of 2011, our community had grown to four hundred. By Easter that following year, we were a rowdy, rousing body of eight hundred and fifty new friends.

I tell you this because churches in San Francisco don't normally, well, work. I mean, of course there are amazing churches in SF with pastors who are some of the best and most caring people you'll ever meet—but the City has been known to eat more than a few new churches alive. You can blame it on Jim Jones, who started a church that turned into a cult that turned into one of the biggest mass suicides in US history. (By the way, they didn't drink Kool-Aid; it was Flavor Aid.) Or you can blame Dan White, the conservative, religious San Francisco politician who ran on family values and then murdered Harvey Milk, the first openly gay man to hold public office in California.

There are a million other factors. But the fact is that when we moved to San Francisco, it was known as a graveyard for churches. The place where movements went to die. So my expectations were low. I hoped that after five years or so we would have a church established.

It happened a lot sooner. We began by teaching the gospel of Mark, and we did this for a simple reason: I wanted people in our community to meet Jesus. That may not sound like a very radical goal for a pastor, but for us it did have an element of risk. Our community seemed to be composed partly of people who grew up in the Bay Area and had never heard what the real Jesus was all about, and partly of refugees from evangelical Christianity who grew up with a very limited picture of Jesus. So I knew our church needed to meet—and to be changed by—the living Jesus we encounter in the pages of Scripture and in life together.

Over the next year and a half we dove deep into the narrative waters of Mark. People loved it. People were shocked and delighted to meet Jesus, whether again or for the first time. People invited their friends and family. People talked about Jesus all the time. Our numbers were growing, but more importantly people were excited and falling in love with Jesus. Jesus! Every pastor's dream.

The problem was that we were still sinning our brains out.

Churchgoers sinning? I know, I know—a real shocker. Of *course* we were still sinning. No one is righteous—not a single one of us! At another level, however, I was surprised. The pervasive and ongoing reality of sin caused me to ask questions. What was the point of meeting the real Jesus if doing so couldn't transform the real sin in our lives? Were we stuck in an endless cycle of failure?

In other words, now that we've been undragoned, how do we live life?

I know what I thought about doing right away. I thought about ending my sermons with punchy, relevant application points. Lists, even. "Don't do this, don't do that. Don't love him, don't love her. Don't drink this, don't touch that." I wanted to make sure we knew the rules. I even started to dust off my youth-pastor hat and considered asking people to start wearing purity rings and signing pledges.

That may sound silly, but don't we all do that? Don't we gravitate toward rules as ways of defining ourselves and measuring ourselves against other people?

At that time I was reading through some of the letters written to the first Christian churches in Corinth, Rome, Ephesus, and Philippi. And when I reached the letter to the church in Colossae, written by the apostle Paul around 62 CE, something clicked—specifically in the transition between chapters 2 and 3, in which Paul addressed the tension he saw between *knowing* Jesus and *living* like Jesus. The difficulty he identified sounded eerily similar to what I was seeing.

He began with a list of rules—"Do not handle! Do not taste! Do not touch!"[3]—but as I read on, the paradigm suddenly shifted. Paul revealed to the Colossians a shocking conclusion: those rules "lack any value in restraining" sin.[4]

Maybe I needed to rethink this! The "do not handle, do not touch" approach I was leaning toward was a popular philosophy in the young church in Colossae. Theologians call it *asceticism*, and it basically posits that in order to come into fullness, or maturity, or to experience all that life with God has to offer, a believer must strictly follow a lengthy list of harsh rules and regulations designed to keep the body and its passions in check.

Keeping the sinful passions of my church in check was exactly what I wanted to do. But Scripture was telling me that rules would be of no use.

When we want to live into our new identities in Christ, we confront this same issue. The things we want can't be accomplished by adding rules about holy behavior! Making such rules speaks only to the environment *around* us, rather than to our hearts, and Jesus teaches us that it is from our hearts that our actions flow.

God absolutely desires that we be holy. We're given new identities for a reason. But there *has* to be a better way than trying to use our willpower to submit to external rules.

And there is.

SELF-HELP

Recently while flying home from Portland, I had my nose buried in a book, and the bright yellow dust jacket caught the flight attendant's eye. She asked me what I was reading. Looking up, I tried to formulate an answer that made sense. "So," I said, "it's this book about culture and ... um ... society and consumerism ... and um ... trying to avoid the constant messages that get bombarded on us every day that ... ah ... define who we are."

Eloquent, right? But all things considered—not bad!

The flight attendant looked at me happily. "Oh!" she chirped. "A self-help book!"

Without really thinking, I replied, "No, not *self*-help—because it says that the only way you can find who you really are is by losing yourself in Jesus."

Her smile cracked. "Okay," she said. "Buh-bye."

Absolutely *all* of us are into self-help. If I'd told her that it *was* a self-help book, she probably would have asked for a quick tip, a quick fix, a quick assurance that she could make her life better if she could just manage to get the right information.

Maybe I could have told her to mute the commercials whenever she's watching television and to repeat a positive phrase to herself—instead of *buy a new car buy a new car* she'd be getting the message *I am unique and special I am unique and special*. And she probably would have tried that.

Not because she's different or more gullible than the rest of us, but precisely because she's just like the rest of us. We *all* want life to be better, and we've been trained to think that it can be better—if only we get the right tips for how to help ourselves.

So I could have told her to eat more spinach, or think about the color yellow before going to sleep, or set her clocks seven minutes ahead, and chances are she would have responded with something like, "Thanks—I'll write that down. I'm totally going to try that when I get home!"

Another tip, another rule, another goal that's up to us to achieve. We try, try, try.

And when we inevitably fail, we assume it's because we didn't try the right thing. We didn't follow the procedure or stick with it long enough or use sufficient willpower. That's why we're open to considering all options available for getting things right the next time, because we're loath to keep failing.

However, there is one option we don't like to consider: that we don't *have* any options left.

As soon as we remove *doing* from the equation of life's identity, we freak out. That message runs counter to everything we hear and everything we've been taught. As soon as we understand that it's not what we *do* that primarily matters in our relationship with God, but who we already *are* in Christ, we can hardly believe it.

When something sounds too good to be true, many of us tune it out. We assume it must be false. Life doesn't work like that, does it? It can't be that easy, can it?

God is relentless, however, and He continues to call out to us. He continues to speak over our lives, just as He did for His Son, Jesus, at the Jordan River, telling us in no uncertain terms that we are His beloved children who bring Him pleasure simply by existing.

Before God tells us what to do, in other words, God tells us who we are.

A BETTER WAY

There is a better way than trying to use our willpower to submit to external rules. This better way is actually the thrust of the whole New Testament, from Jesus onward, and Paul was particularly clear about it in the third chapter of Colossians. Check out the first ten verses.

> Since, then, you have been raised with Christ,
> set your hearts on things above, where Christ is,
> seated at the right hand of God. Set your minds
> on things above, not on earthly things. *For you*

died, and your life is now hidden with Christ in God. When *Christ, who is your life,* appears, then you also will appear with him in glory.

Put to death, *therefore,* whatever belongs to your earthly nature: sexual immorality, impurity, lust, evil desires and greed, which is idolatry. Because of these, the wrath of God is coming. *You used to* walk in these ways, in the life you once lived. *But now* you must also rid yourselves of all such things as these: anger, rage, malice, slander, and filthy language from your lips. Do not lie to each other, *since you have taken off* your old self with its practices *and have put on* the new self, which is being renewed in knowledge in the image of its Creator.

What was Paul getting at? If trying to rule ourselves with "don't do this and don't do that" doesn't work to make us holier, what does?

Becoming who we are.

Look again at the ten verses above. Remember that Paul, in the previous chapter, made the stunning statement that rules "lack any value in restraining" our sin. However, there is a way that works, and it has everything to do with the truest thing about us—our identity in Christ.

This was basically Paul's message in each letter. John and Peter got into the act in their letters as well. Jesus said the same thing when He told His followers that they were the salt of the earth and the light of the world. He didn't tell them they could be salt and light *if* they kept certain rules—rather, that they were *already* salt and light because of their connection to Him.

What the believers in Colossae had failed to recognize was that they had already received everything needed to live as sanctified disciples of Jesus.

Does that problem sound familiar?

You are loved by God, accepted by God, and put in right relationship with God. It's not by your own doing, or because you have the right family, or because you have the right education, or because you have the right desires or attractions, or because you have the right job. It's because of the sacrificial death and resurrection of Jesus. Because of *that* your life is hidden with Christ—and nothing can take you away. You belong to God.

If you have placed your trust in Christ, that's who you are.

And our call, then, is to *become* who we are—to live out the truth of this truest thing about us. There are many true things about you—about what you do and have and desire—but only one thing is the truest.

Whatever you believe is the truest will be your functioning identity. And if you are a follower of Jesus, that identity is safely secured in the God who loves you. Learning to become who you are and live out of this identity is a process. As pastor Tim Keller pointed out,

> Identity is a complex set of layers, for we are many things. Our occupation, ethnic identity, etc., are part of who we are. But we assign different values to these components and thus Christian maturing is a process in which the most fundamental layer of our identity becomes our self-understanding as a new creature in Christ along with all our privileges in him.[5]

Trusting in Jesus means that you *do* have a new identity. You already have it, and you didn't have to earn it. It can't be taken from you. And living out of it is the secret to living toward Jesus.

Christ *is* your life.

Henri Nouwen has never changed my life more profoundly than when he wrote this sentence: "From the moment we claim the truth of being the Beloved, we are faced with the call to become who we are."

Become who you are. That transformed my whole conception of identity and belonging.

But the phrase also sounds tangled, troubled. What does it actually *mean*?

It means this: You belong to Christ. You are hidden with Christ. You are God's beloved. That is the truest thing about you, and therefore you must become that preexisting truth if you are to avoid becoming a lie. These things are true about you—now become what is already true.

Drive this truth, this identity, so deep into your psyche, your personhood, your sense of self-worth, that this truth becomes your fountainhead, the source of your life.

Become who you are.

INDICATIVES

Christ is your new identity. Christ is your life. But let me ask you a question: *is* Christ your life?

That's a loaded question. I think most of us, if we were being honest, would say something like, "No, Christ isn't my *life* … but I want Him to be."

And what if I asked you to explain: why isn't Christ your life?

Then you might go into more detail about your life and your choices. You might admit that you still do what *you* want to do sometimes, or that you don't pray enough, or that you haven't forgiven a certain person even though you know you should. With your sin and failure so apparent, so ever present, you might wonder how you could *ever* claim that Christ is truly your life.

Yet always the important caveat: that you *want* Him to be ...

However, Paul proclaimed something much different from that in Colossians 3. He stated that Christ *is* your life. He is. Fact. Done deal.

He did not say that Christ is your life if you accomplish this, give away that, and forgive those. No. None of that. Paul stated, qualification free, that Christ is your life.

This kind of statement in Scripture is called an *indicative*— something that has already been indicated or declared about you as a fact, a truth.

Indicatives aren't the only kind of statement in Scripture, however. There are also *imperatives*. An imperative is something we are supposed to do, phrased as a command or a direction. It might sound dry to talk about types of speech, but it is hugely important for this reason: *when we confuse indicatives with imperatives, we sabotage our ability to live in our new identities.*

Colossians 3 is full of indicatives. You have been raised with Christ. You died, and your life is now hidden with Christ. Christ is your life. All of these things are declared about you as *facts that are already true.*

The minute we hear these as instructions for *us* to accomplish—as imperatives—we hear a lie. Some of us have the feeling that *all* we hear in church or around Christians are imperatives. Commands that threaten our freedom. And some of us church types actually love imperatives, but for selfish reasons. See, if we keep all the commands and rules, we can chart our progress toward holiness and present ourselves as righteous people.

But both of those approaches are wrong!

Here's why. Every imperative in Scripture is based on an indicative. In other words, we're never asked to do something until we're told something true about who we are.

Dig this heavy-duty thought from Sinclair Ferguson:

> So often in our preaching our indicatives [truths] are not strong enough, great enough, holy enough, or gracious enough to sustain the power of the imperatives [commands]. And so our teaching on holiness becomes a whip or a rod to beat our people's backs because we've looked at the New Testament and that's all we ourselves have seen. We've seen our

own failure and we've seen the imperatives to holiness and *we've lost sight of the great indicatives of the gospel that sustain those imperatives.*[6]

Yes. That.

The truths of the gospel support and sustain the commands of the gospel. If we do not first understand the truth about who we are—the truest thing about us—we will be crushed by the weight of the commands.

Jesus always tells us who we are before He ever tells us what to do, because Jesus knows two things about those who will choose to follow Him. First, He's asking the impossible. And second, He specializes in making the impossible possible.

Let's take this for a test drive. Think about some of the heaviest commands we're given in Scripture. The imperatives are always based on an indicative that is already true about us.

You will flee sexual immorality—true, but not before you are reminded that your body is a temple of the Holy Spirit. Christ is in you. That's *who you are*, so *because* of that, flee sexual immorality. Do nothing out of selfish ambition—true, but not before you are reminded that the mind of Christ, the ultimate humble servant, is in you. *That's who you are*, so *because* of that, act in humility. You will forgive your enemies—true, but not before you are reminded that you have been forgiven. The death of Jesus has washed away every sin. *That's who you are*, so *because* of that, forgive your enemies.

This paradigm isn't found only in the New Testament. Think of the greatest list of rules in all of human history, the Ten Commandments. How does it begin? "I am the LORD your God, who brought you out of Egypt."[7] That's identity, ladies and gentlemen. You were slaves, but now you're free, and because of *that*, live like *this*.

We simply cannot become who we should be. It's impossible. The only thing we can become is who we are.

It's the high and beautiful gospel indicatives that sustain the gospel imperatives. In Christ, we can become who we are.

EVERYWHERE

You can read this truth—indicatives before imperatives—for yourself. Put on your become-who-you-are glasses and read these verses from 1 Peter.

Here's the imperative:

> Dear friends, I *urge* you, as foreigners and exiles, to *abstain* from sinful desires, which

wage war against your soul. *Live* such good lives among the pagans that, though they accuse you of doing wrong, they may see your good deeds and glorify God on the day he visits us.

And here's the indicative:

But you *are* a chosen people, a royal priest-hood, a holy nation, God's special possession, that you may declare the praises of him who called you out of darkness into his wonderful light. *Once you were* not a people, but *now you are* the people of God; once you had not received mercy, but *now you have received* mercy.

Guess which comes first? The second set of verses comes from 1 Peter 2:9–10. And the first set of verses comes from 1 Peter 2:11–12.

Identity statements are everywhere. Find a command, and you'll find somewhere near it a truth about who you are.

This is what we needed to learn in my church. This is what the Bible is getting at when it talks about living into the Christian life. And when I started to preach that story, I had a steady stream of people coming up to me after sermons.

And they were *mad.*

Angry because some of them had been Christians for a long time—and no one had ever told them this. No one had ever let them know that our actions flow from our identity, and not the other way around. No one had ever shown them how Scripture builds every command on the foundation of the truth of our identity in Christ.

I told them I was discovering this along with them, which is how this book was born.

TO BE LOVED

Recently one of my best friends texted me out of the blue.

I love you so much. More than you'll ever know.

That was the whole text. I was doing something totally normal, trying to eat a burrito and read the news on my phone. And suddenly a well-known voice from another city interrupted me with a wonderful message.

I was shocked. We don't normally text things like that to each other. But I was also delighted. I mean, if you want to talk about a message of affirmation and support and flat-out love, you can't do much better. I smiled a big smile and read the text a few more times. I felt a warm glow that wasn't just the burrito I was scarfing. I was basking in the knowledge that this friend chose to take time out of his busy day to randomly send me such an affirming message.

And then I started thinking. Why did he text me that? Why that day? Why those words? *What had I done that he liked that made him decide to text me?*

I wondered if he'd read something I'd written and wanted to let me know how much he appreciated me. Or maybe some-one had told him how well my church was doing, and so my friend texted me to be like, *Dude, you're doing good, and I love you.* Or maybe I was just being particularly awesome that week.

No matter the reason, my line of thinking was inexorably lead-ing me to a clear conclusion. My friend loved me because, in some sense and for some reason, *I deserved to be loved.*

Isn't that what we always do? We take whatever approval we receive and wrap it around what we do, what we have, and what we desire—in other words, we wrap it around our com-posite idea of our own identity. (The reverse is true as well: we take whatever disapproval we receive and attribute it to our own failings, lacks, and issues.)

We ask a simple question: why does my boss/friend/lover/ child/pastor like me?

Then we give a simple answer: it must be because I deserve it.

"We are loved *because* ..." That sentence is the biggest single failing of our perception of identity. The reason that's wrong is because we try to earn love. We try to base our identity on what we do, what we have, what we desire. We try to deserve love from others and God. But we never can.

The contrast between God's way and our way is stark.

Our paradigm is this: I'm loved *because* ...

Since that's our paradigm, we try to do things that continue to make us lovable. We do what others want, or what we think they want. We put on a smiling face and never let others see our failures. Not even God. Because who loves a failure? Would my friend have texted me that day if I'd spent the whole previous week screwing up?

But here's God's paradigm for us: I'm loved. *Therefore* ...

That single word of difference changes everything. Our identity as beloved children of God is not dependent on a condition but secure from the moment we turn to Him. The moment our lives are hidden in Christ. God's *therefores* are always built on the unconditional truth that we are loved.

When the Father spoke over Jesus at the Jordan River, say-ing, "This is My beloved Son,"[8] the words came before Jesus had done anything to earn that love. There was no *because* that day—only a *therefore* as Jesus was empowered to live into His new identity.

Watch as Jesus shows how this paradigm functions in real life, even in seemingly impossible situations.

LIVE OUT OF WHO YOU ARE

"Whore!"

He spat the word, his face red and veins bulging on his fore-head. Grabbing the woman by the arm, he flung her to the ground, where she looked up from bloody knees. Still breath-ing hard, the man, a religious scholar dressed in the finest robes, turned his attention to the young man directly in front of him.

The young man, surrounded by an attentive crowd, had until that moment been teaching the gathered crowd from the Scriptures. He had a dark beard, olive skin, a homespun robe, and eyes that seemed like the calm at the center of the brew-ing storm.

The sun was just breaking over the white stones of the temple wall, and the shadows of the woman's accusers spread across the dirt from one side of the temple court to the other. The young man stood up and looked at her.

She was clearly guilty of adultery. He knew it, she knew it, and everyone watching knew it.

The religious leader looked around, making sure that everyone was watching him. He straightened his robe, cleared his throat, and blustered at Jesus of Nazareth. "Teacher, this woman is an adulterer—we caught her in the very act! Moses, in the law, gives orders to stone such persons. What do *you* say?"

The temple courtyard was silent, save for the muffled sobs of the woman, as everyone strained to hear Jesus' response. In the hush, Jesus bent down and began to write on the ground with His finger. Was He thinking? Making a point? Stalling?

As the silence stretched, the religious leader became agitated. Searching for strength in the eyes of the other religious leaders behind him, he turned again to Jesus and tried to ask his question again, this time in a louder voice. "Teacher, this woman was caught in the act—"

Jesus finally straightened and looked at the religious leader, cutting his question off midsentence. "The sinless ones among you," He said, locking eyes with each of the religious leaders in turn, "go first. Throw the stone." In the silence that followed, Jesus bent down once again and wrote in the dirt.

It was the sound of sandals shuffling away that made the woman first lift her head. Hardly daring to hope, she turned to look at the men who had dragged her there. The oldest ones were already halfway across the courtyard, while the younger ones were beginning to mutter curses and shift on their feet. The rising sun filled the courtyard with light and colored the woman's face with a soft glow. As the temple brightened, she watched each of the men turn and walk away. Soon only their leader remained, clenching and unclenching his fists. Then, with a low growl, he spun on his heels and stalked from the temple.

That was when the woman heard a voice behind her. It was the rabbi they called Jesus. "Where are they? Does no one condemn you?"

She could hardly believe the simple truth of her reply. "No one."

"Neither do I," said Jesus, the beginnings of a smile lighting His dark eyes. "Go on your way. And from now on," He continued, looking into her eyes with a kindness she had never known, "don't sin."[9]

THE WORST AND BEST NEWS POSSIBLE

Remember the way, in *The Voyage of the Dawn Treader*, Eustace tries to remove his own scales? And how he fails?

What Eustace gets right is that he needs to be transformed. The truest thing about him is that he is a boy trapped inside a dragon, and so his scales must be removed. What Eustace gets wrong, however, is the method. He sinks his own claws into his own scales, hoping to remove them and reveal the boy beneath. It's self-surgery, and it fails.

Just as it does when we try it.

Transformation doesn't begin with cleaning up and getting our acts together. It begins with meeting Jesus. When we do that, we are identified with Jesus and given new identities—identities based on *His* righteousness and standing with God.

And that is how we become who we are. Not by our own effort or achievement, but by virtue of our being hidden in Christ. When Christ is our life, then we—just like Christ—are God's beloved.

But what does that mean? Here's Nouwen again:

> Being the Beloved expresses the core truth of our existence.... Though the experience of being the Beloved has never been completely absent from my life, I never claimed it as my core truth. I kept running around it in large or small circles, always looking for someone or something able to convince me of my Belovedness. I kept refusing to hear the voice that speaks from the very depth of my being that says: "You are my Beloved, on you my favor rests." That voice has always been there, but it seems that I was much more eager to listen to other, louder voices saying: "Prove that you are worth something; do something relevant, spectacular, or powerful, and then you will earn the love you so desire."[10]

We keep coming back to this because we keep *needing* to come back to this. Don't we keep skirting the issue, running around it in "large or small circles," pretending like we're engaging the heart of our existence while really remaining at a safe distance?

Are you as sick as I am of the endless cycle of self-improvement that doesn't improve a thing?

It isn't easy to understand God's love for us, in large part because we can't accept how simple it is. The fact is that most of us cannot imagine a relationship that isn't based—at least in part and at certain times—on quid pro quo. This even happens in the best of relationships. I love my wife truly, deeply, madly, and forever, but do I sometimes work at something a bit harder because I know she'll appreciate it? Yes.

A story I once read helped me picture the upside-down orientation of God's relationship with us. In our daily lives, *adult* is typically a compliment and *childish* is typically pejorative. But what if that isn't a helpful way to picture our relationship with God?

Imagine a young boy who wants to buy his father a birthday present. He knows his father likes to read, so the boy decides to buy a book. On his way home from school, the boy stops at a bookshop and finds a title he knows his father will like. When he goes to buy it, however, he discovers he has nowhere near enough money.

The boy is undeterred. That evening he asks his father if he can have thirteen dollars, without telling his father what the money is for. The boy's father looks into his son's eyes, weighs the situation, and takes the money from his wallet. The boy receives the money, carefully folds it, and leaves the room without a word.

Later that week, after dinner one night, the boy asks his parents if he can get something from his room. He returns to the table with a package wrapped in newspaper comics and heavily taped. He places it in front of his father on the table.

"Open it."

The boy's father rips apart a long strip of newsprint, revealing the cover of a book. He looks up at his son, and his son is watching him back. The father slides the rest of the wrapping paper off the book, sets the book gently on the table, and beckons to his son. When his son crosses to the other side of the table, the father wraps his left arm around his boy. The father's right hand fits the curve of his son's cheek, gently pulling that small head close to his chest, where he will be able to catch the scent of his boy's hair. The present remains on the table—the father already has a copy of the same book on his shelf.

"This is just what I wanted," he says into his son's hair. "Thank you."[11]

What do we make of such a story?

We may be tempted to conclude that the son's gift doesn't count for much. Since the father already had the book, he certainly didn't need another one—not to mention that the father was the one who paid for his own pointless gift in the first place. Or we may be tempted to conclude that the father isn't genuinely pleased with his gift and is merely offering lip service to his son by thanking him. He's trying to make his boy feel good, but the father's compliments are all surface and no substance. Or perhaps we just chuckle, seeing this as a funny tale of fatherhood with no deeper meaning.

The story's core is more complicated and more beautiful. When we understand that this is a picture of our relationship to our Father in heaven, something emerges, like a figure walking toward us out of the fog.

It is the feeling of hope.

We don't, after all, need to impress God sufficiently to warrant His love and approval. If we did, we would live our lives in a constant state of trembling anxiety, wondering if *this* gift or *that* gift is the right one to earn us a fatherly smile. Some of us do live that way. However, God is waiting to pull us close, to bless us, no matter what gift we bring. And any gift we bring—our time, our love, our scholarship, our art, our relationships, our job—*was given to us by God in the first place.*

The prophet Isaiah once said that when we try to present our best, most righteous actions to God, they're no better than bloodied rags used by a woman during her period. If you think that's a graphic image today, dial up your reaction by a factor of ten and you'll start to have an idea of what Isaiah was getting at with his original audience.

Yet this leads us not to despair ... but to hope. The point is not that we will never *earn* God's approval with our gifts, although that is true. The point, rather, is that we don't *need* to earn God's approval with our gifts, *because when God looks at us in Christ, He already approves of us.*

Look—God has given us everything. *Literally* everything. From the mix of oxygen and nitrogen and carbon dioxide we breathe to the ability to taste, and from our capacity to form relationships to the fact that the sun is exactly the correct distance from Earth. And then we show up and do something godly. We begin to give sacrificially of our time or adopt an orphan. *Hey, God*, we say, *check me out!*

God already has. He checked you out when you were still a blob of doubling-every-few-hours cells, and He loved you. And later, before you could even form a coherent thought— before you'd done anything more praiseworthy than spit up and sleep—God still loved you. Just as He loves you today.

Does God love it when we're righteous? Absolutely. But we're *only* righteous when we're covered by the righteousness that Jesus gives us—and never righteous on our own.

Are you starting to feel the truth of the truest thing about you?

The call to *become who we are* is the only claim on our lives that matters.

We cannot change who we are, and that is the worst and the best news imaginable.

Worst because there is nothing we can do—not one single thing—that will make us better people. And best because despite that, God calls us beloved. God delights in us. God saved us while we were still a long way off.

A WAY FORWARD
BECOME WHO YOU ARE

Sin is building your self-worth on anything other than God.

Søren Kierkegaard

LISTS

The call of the Christian life is to become who you are. Remember Nouwen's words? Once you claim the truth for yourself that you are God's beloved, your call in life is to become who you are. You are God's beloved. You are in Christ. You are a new creation.

And that only scratches the surface of who you *are*.

You are redeemed from slavery to sin. (Rom. 3:24; 8:23)

You are reconciled to God. (2 Cor. 5:18–20)

You are forgiven of all your sins. (Col. 2:13)

You are washed clean. (Isa. 1:18)

You are free. (Rom. 6:14; 8:1–4; Gal. 5:1–4)

You are adopted by God. (Gal. 3:26–4:7; Eph. 1:4–5)

You are accepted by God. (Eph. 1:6)

You have become a child of God. (John 3:3, 7)

You are justified by Jesus. (Rom. 4; 5:1)

You are glorified with Jesus. (Rom. 4:17; 8:18; 8:30; Col. 3:4)

You are united to Jesus. (Col. 2:9–10)

You possess every spiritual blessing. (Eph. 1:3)

You are delivered from the power of darkness. (Col. 1:13; 2 Cor. 4:3–4)

You join the people of God. (1 Pet. 2:9)

You smell good to God. (2 Cor. 2:15)

You are granted access to God. (Heb. 4:16; 10:10–20)

You are in God. (1 Thess. 1:1)

God the Father is in you. (Eph. 4:6)

You are in the Son. (Rom. 8:1)

The Son is in you. (John 14:20)

You are in the Spirit. (Rom. 8:9)

The Spirit is in you. (1 Cor. 2:12)

You are whole in Christ. (Col. 2:10)[1]

When you are in Christ, you *are* that. Now how do you *become* that?

A man who had recently become a Christian asked me this during a meeting before he was to be baptized: "Am I being transformed and renewed by God Himself, or am I converting my lifestyle to the social norms and expectations of a group of people who claim to have the keys to salvation?"

Smart man. But I'm smart too, so I asked *him* a question: "Why don't you talk to our associate pastor?"

In the end, we had a thought-provoking conversation, and his question caused me to dig as deeply as I could into the nature of Christian transformation.

Is Christian transformation—what the Bible calls "sanctification" and the process of "becoming like Christ"—something we *do*? If it *is* something we do, aren't we back at square one, responsible to work for and earn our own salvation? And if sanctification is something we do, what exactly does it require? Are we doing something for or with God, or are we simply converting our lifestyle to match the social norms of our particular denomination or Christian tradition?

This is the point where most people hear "The List." (Not the list on the previous pages, unfortunately.)

It's the list of what to do and not to do. Most churches have them. Some are written; some are unsaid. The list goes something like this: go to church once (or thrice) a week, don't live with your boyfriend or girlfriend before you get married, stop smoking and drinking, forget what you learned at university (especially in the sciences), be nice to people (so that when they ask why you are so nice, you can tell them about your church and about Jesus), start voting for conservatives, buy shirts that steal cool secular designs but combine them with clever Christian slogans (sorry, low blow), start doing something along the lines of social justice, and start giving money to the church.

That covers it, more or less. That's what we're supposed to be doing, we're told. And there are many who think that this is the sum and essence of Christianity.

Now, some of the items on that list are actually found in a list of vices Paul himself used in the New Testament letters. For example, in Colossians 3:5 Paul wrote that believers should "put to death, therefore, whatever belongs to your earthly nature: sexual immorality, impurity, lust, evil desires and greed, which is idolatry."

Here's the strange part. Just a few sentences before that list in Colossians, as we saw in our previous chapter, Paul said *not* to add lists to what Christ has done because they don't help us restrain our sinful desires. There is a subtle distinction here that is vitally important. It goes back to that gentleman's question to me: is *God* transforming me, or am I simply becoming a cultural Christian?

The question really is: what's shaping us as followers of Jesus?

To Paul, the answer was our new identity *in Christ*.

The difference between the "do not taste, do not touch" lists Paul condemned and Paul's list of instructions to "put to death ..." is found in the very pregnant word *therefore*.

So what's *therefore* there for?

By using the word *therefore*, Paul was not using a "list" to transform us but instead was appealing to our new selves in Christ as the prerequisite and foundation for *all* action we take as Christians. Lists, no matter how noble, do not restrain our sinful natures. However, our identity in Christ *gives* us new natures into which we can live.

Remember how we talked about the Ten Commandments, the list to end all lists, and how those commandments do the same thing? Before the Israelites were given a list of how to live godly lives, they were reminded of their identity: "I am the LORD your God, who brought you out of Egypt, out of the land of slavery."[2] Who they are is the *basis* for how they will live, not the other way around. It's as if God is saying, "Your life in Me will look a certain way *because* of My deliverance, My redeeming love, and My provision for you—*because of who you are.*"

That's the *therefore* tradition Paul was working with. When we divorce the commands of God—what we called indicatives a little earlier—from who Jesus is and our identity in Him, the commands and lists become religious impossibilities.

We need to understand that a list isn't as much about *doing* as it is about *being who we are*.

Let's explore that.

HOLIED

In the Old Testament, whenever an item was placed in the temple, it was set apart for God. Devoted to God's purposes only, present in that place for God's glory only. It could have been a stunning work of art, like a tapestry woven with gold and silver thread, or it could have been as simple as a candlestick. But no matter what it was, it could be used only for God's purposes.

In other words, it was *holied*. The physical way of representing this was by anointing it with oil. Anointing an object or a person meant it was to be holied and set apart for God's purposes.

If you are a follower of Jesus, *you* are holied.

So when Paul wrote to the Corinthians, a church that was starting to look more like their progressively sinful city than the church of God, he said, "To the church of God in Corinth, to those *holied* in Christ Jesus and called to be his holy people ..."[3]

Holied. Holy.

You are holied. Set apart for God and devoted to His purposes. And because you are in Christ, because you are God's
beloved, because God's Spirit lives in you, you are also called
to *be* holy.

Paul was writing to the Corinthians with the motivation to
help Christians in Corinth gain a better grasp of their true
identity and reflect it in their behavior inside and outside the
church.[4]

Christ gives you His righteousness and holiness. If you are in
Christ, that righteousness and that holiness are yours. Those
things are who you are. Now *be* who you are.

Because of your new identity, you are invited to see your
entire world in a different light. Invited to live a new narrative. So sex looks different. Money looks different. So does
power and work and family and wisdom and love. You live
in San Francisco or New York or Omaha, but you are not,
strictly speaking, a native of those places. You are a native of
God's kingdom, and from that kingdom the view of the world
is much different.

A boat must be *in* the water if it is to fulfill its identity as a
boat—yet a boat cannot function if too much of that water is
in *it*.

You are set apart. You are holied, and you are called to *be* holy.

EVERYTHING IN ITS PROPER PLACE

According to Kwame Anthony Appiah's book *The Ethics of Identity*, there are two rival understandings of modern identity.

One involves the process of discovery. You discover yourself by reflecting or paying careful attention to an authentic identity that is within you. Your true self is who you already are.

Or you invent and assemble your identity. You make up a self from scratch, compiling all of your favorite things to make a life worth living. Your true self is whoever you want to be.

Appiah argued that both approaches are wrong.[5] The first is wrong because it suggests that there is *no* role for creativity in selfhood—that the self is fixed by our natures and can only be discovered, not modified or changed. And the second is wrong because it suggests that there are no limits. A tree *cannot* become a cow, or even a vine. Our self-identities must have limits, and to think otherwise is silly.

What's the alternative?

That parts of both are true—and this is exactly what we see in Scripture. We take part in the act of becoming who we are, certainly, just as we are called to love God and neighbor with all our heart, soul, mind, and strength. That takes creativity and participation. At the same time, we can't choose to be simply *anything* we want and *poof!* find ourselves transformed.

The authentic identity inside us is the *imago Dei*—the same for each of God's created children, yet different for every unique individual.

Unless we search for our identity *in Christ*, our search will be in vain:

> One's search for self ultimately is fruitless because it seeks to *find* that which can only be given by another. In short, we may seek self-identity and hope to find ourselves, but the hoped-for result never occurs through our own efforts. *We seek ourselves, but are finally found!* One's identity is the gift of another's love.[6]

Identity in Christ starts with believing something about Jesus and *then* believing something about ourselves in light of what we believe about Jesus.

What is this something?

Near the beginning of his letter to the followers of Jesus in Colossae, Paul penned a lengthy description of Jesus. Many of our modern Bibles call this section "The Preeminence of Christ," and that's a fitting title. We are familiar, just as Paul's first hearers would have been, with the biography of Jesus— how He came to earth to be born, live a perfect life, teach and heal, be killed on a cross, and ultimately rise from the dead. Paul, however, wanted to rip the frame off that particular portrait and begin adding color and detail out past the edges of the canvas. *Way* out past the edges. Just who is Jesus Christ?

Paul wrote that He is the exact image of God. He is the One who created the entire universe. He is in charge of all things, and all things are held together and sustained by His active power. Not only that, wrote Paul, but Jesus is the head of the church on earth, as well as the preeminent person in all of creation. Because He is all of these things, Jesus was able "to reconcile to himself all things, whether things on earth or things in heaven, by making peace through his blood, shed on the cross."[7]

Now *that's* a high view of Christ. A good moral teacher, as some today like to call Him? Sure—and that covers about one-tenth of 1 percent of His identity.

If this is what we are to first believe about Jesus, what are we to believe about *ourselves*? How does our view of Jesus shape our identity?

Like this: if we begin with Jesus, *every subsequent thing we think or see about ourselves will be seen in the light of His truth.*

It's not about right belief, exactly—more like rightly *ordered* belief. We begin with Jesus, for that is the only way we can truly see ourselves. The truth of Jesus is the genuine article by which we can call out the lies of our false identities. The truth of Jesus is also the truest truth, by which we can rightly see the less true things about our identity. You may be addicted, but that is not the truest thing about you. You may be a husband, but that is not the truest thing about you. You may be single, but that is not the truest thing about you. You can see that these things are lies, or that they are true without being the truest, only when you start with the preeminence of Christ.

The French philosopher Blaise Pascal put it this way:

> Not only do we only know God through Jesus Christ, but we only know ourselves through Jesus Christ: we only know life and death through Jesus Christ. Apart from Jesus Christ we cannot know the meaning of our life or of our death, of God, or ourselves.[8]

When it comes to our identity, to knowing the truest thing about us, knowing Christ first is everything.

AS IF NOT

What does any of this look like in the real world? What does becoming who we are and our new identity in Christ have to do with, well, *living*?

For most of us, disengaging from life isn't an option. Yes, there are people who leave everything behind and become hermits of some sort. And there are those who choose to join like-minded groups that help them live out their new identities, such as a monastic order or an intentional community. The vast majority of people who choose to follow Jesus, however, do so inside the context of a job, a neighborhood, a family, a group of friends, a church, and so on. Like before.

We still operate and live each day as individuals—but there *is* a paradigm shift.

Remember how we began chapter 6? When we are in Christ, there is a top-to-bottom reimagining of our entire lives. The way we live changes, radically.

Look at the provocative way Paul said it in the seventh chapter of his first letter to the Corinthians:

> What I mean, brothers and sisters, is that the
> time is short. From now on those who have
> wives should live *as if they do not*; those who

mourn, *as if they did not*; those who are happy, *as if they were not*; those who buy something, *as if it were not* theirs to keep.[9]

What in the world does that mean? If I'm married to Ash, I should live as if I'm not? That doesn't seem to make a whole lot of sense.

The only way we *can* make sense of it is to understand Paul's comment in light of our identity in Christ. That, in fact, is the point of his whole letter. What's going on is a practical consequence of reimagining life in relation to our new identities. Most of us still live life like we did before we met Jesus, from staying married to staying in a job to staying in an apartment. Of course we do. And at the same time, our relationship to all of that is reimagined. It's like looking at a beautiful cityscape under a bright summer sun ... and then putting on a pair of polarized sunglasses. We see all the same things as before, but everything looks different.

In the verse I quoted above, Paul was not discouraging us from buying and selling. He was not discouraging marriage. He was not discouraging mourning or being happy.

Rather, he was *encouraging* us to realize that we do all these things differently now. We don't do them because we find our identity in them. Our identity is in Christ, and that changes everything. So much so, in fact, that even if I'm married to

Ash, my marriage can't be my identity because my identity is in Christ.

So we buy, but not to possess a life or a new identity.

We can marry, but not because the other person will "complete us" or make us perfectly happy.

We will mourn, but not like those without hope.

We are happy, but we are not slaves to happiness like those who pursue pleasure as an identity.

We can be single. But not single like those who have no family, because we are in Christ, and in Christ's body we have a whole new family, the church.

We live now, but we live *as if not* to gather an identity from any of these things.

We are all these same things—but not in the same way. We are all these same things—but not as if we are gathering an identity from them. Our new identity in Christ causes us to reimagine all of life. Not to stop living life, but rather to work and relate and play *as if* those things are not the truest things about us. They're not the source of our identity anymore. We live *as if* these things do not determine our existence, because that power belongs only to Christ.

That is why, after beginning to follow Christ, our lives can sometimes *look* similar—we remain married, or we remain at our job, or we remain in the same city—yet be transformed from the inside out.

What are the net results of this paradigm shift? We can finally *enjoy* all these same things. Perhaps you're like me and tend to be disappointed easily. Whenever you purchase something you think it will "solve your universe." Whenever you date someone you think, *This person is the one who will complete me.* When you get that career advancement you think, *This will bring me everything I've always wanted.* Maybe you don't say these things out loud, but you believe them. Until always—inevitably—that thing or person or job can't handle the weight of your expectations, and you are once again let down.

The *as if not* paradigm frees you to enjoy the thing for what it is. A car just becomes transportation, not the thing that will bring ultimate driving pleasure. A relationship can be a wonderful God-given form of human connection that may or may not lead to marriage. Your job can provide you with satisfaction, but it doesn't have to save your soul.

Because of who we are in Christ, we can have things without those things having us. We can live *as if not.*

This changes everything.

THE FREEDOM TO REST

One of the most countercultural ways to live into our identity in Christ is to *take a day off*. That's not as easy as it sounds. Scripture calls this Sabbath, and for us moderns, it's one of the most rejected ideas in the Bible.

Sabbath reminds us that we are loved for who we are, *not* for what we can produce. Sabbath is the real-life practice of finding our identity in Christ, not in what we do or in what we have. It is all too easy for us to allow work to determine our identity. Most of us spend the largest single chunk of our lives working. More than being with friends. More than sleeping. More than pursuing our favorite hobbies. It's no wonder we can get our relationship with work so wrong—it's constantly demanding our time and attention.

Work isn't just ubiquitous in our society. Work was actually designed by God. In the perfection of the garden of Eden, before the fall, the first humans were given work to do. They were asked to accomplish things like naming the animals and tending the various plants that grew there. And after the fall, Scripture makes clear that the mandate to work continues. God asked the Israelite artisans to create a temple for Him. The New Testament is full of instructions and teaching about work. And followers of God are told that they were created *for good works* that—get ready to be shocked—God *prepared for them to do before they were even born*.

But we have a nasty habit of screwing it all up. We take something that is part of our *imago Dei*—the call to work—and make it a source of identity. Or an idol. Or an escape. Or an excuse. Or a source of self-worth. Or the engine of our consumerism.

That's exactly why the only way to understand work properly is to understand the biblical concept of Sabbath. If there is a single idea in this book that is both countercultural *and* incredibly practical, it is this: spend your time differently by taking a Sabbath.

So here's what Sabbath is and what it means. Work, in our society, is about production and achievement. Sabbath is about not producing. Sabbath is about not "achieving" anything.

In the words of Eugene Peterson, Sabbath is about shutting up and showing up. We kill our own agendas, and we show up before God. We lay before Him our week behind and our week ahead; we stop laboring for money, for meaning, for purpose, for image management, for relationship management. Instead we simply *rest*. For a full day we stop trying to produce and let God produce in us. To some that might mean reading, writing, hiking, meditating, painting, taking pictures, surfing ... but it always means prayer. Ceasing from work brings all our anxieties to the surface and confronts us with what we've been running from for the last six days. And in prayer we offer all that to God. We say, *My identity is in You, God. In You.*

Sabbath is about recognizing that, despite what we're told or what we think during our working week, it is *God* who controls and holds everything. Money. Jobs. Relationships. God is the One in charge of these things, not us. We do not make the world go round with our efforts at work. The things we do and the things we have, both possessions and power, can never give us a true identity. And it is when we choose to Sabbath, to climb off the hamster wheel of life and begin to listen, that we hear God affirming our true identities.

You are not a worker—you are My child.

You are not a producer—you are My beloved.

I do not love you because of what you do or what you have, but because of who you are in Christ.

Let me confess something to you. Being a preaching pastor is a hard gig. Every week I am expected to preach a sermon that is inspired, encouraging, convicting, fresh, applicable, and true! And though this perspective may not be based in reality, I feel like I am being judged about my worth every week, based on my sermon.

I don't say this for sympathy but to show you how this idea of Sabbath retrains me to place my identity in *Jesus* and not in my sermon. Every Saturday I Sabbath. I break. I rest. From sundown Friday night to sundown Saturday night I do no work—not even last-minute tweaks to my sermon. This is a hard practice for me. When I wake up Saturday morning, I hear a voice in my head telling me that tomorrow will be when I prove myself, so I'd better be good. And that's exactly why I Sabbath then—to force myself, week after week, to reestablish my identity in Christ.

So I pray something like this: *My identity is not in preaching a good sermon or proving my worth tomorrow, God. My identity is in You.*

Then I have my coffee, go surfing, and hang out with my wife. And I keep praying that prayer.

Sabbath, in the Old Testament, is built on two foundations. The first is creation, and the second is liberation.[10]

In the garden, God began by establishing the pattern of Sabbath. And because we are made in God's image, we, too, are meant to reflect this pattern with our rhythm of work and rest. Then, after the Israelites were rescued from Egypt, God reminded them that they were no longer slaves, and therefore they no longer needed to work seven days a week. In Egypt, there was no option. They had to work—that choice was made for them every day. And their worth came from the amount of bricks they produced.

Does that sound familiar?

When was the last time you put away your phone and computer and television for twenty-four hours? Does the idea of shutting off your email, not checking in at work, and not managing your image on Facebook make you anxious? Are you afraid of not being busy, not producing? Have you ever wondered if work is becoming more than a job for you—becoming a source of identity? When did you last *rest*?

For the Israelites in Egypt, rest was for other people. Rest was for Pharaoh. And when God redeemed and rescued His people from that slavery, He reminded them that rest was for them.

We need this ancient countercultural reality today.

The word *Sabbath* is the Hebrew word *Shabbat*, which simply means "quit." Stop. Take a break. Cool it. The word itself has nothing devout or holy in it. It is a word about time, denoting our nonuse of it, what we usually call wasting time.[11]

Sabbath is not a day off. Did you catch that? *We don't take a Sabbath because we need a day off*. The motivation behind a "day off" is completely utilitarian: to restore strength, increase motivation, reward effort, and keep performance incentives high. The end result of that kind of Sabbath is … more work. Eugene Peterson called that a "bastard sabbath,"[12] and for good reason—it is a corruption of God's intent.

Do you have a fear of not "succeeding"? Do you worry that you'll let others down? Do you worry that if you don't produce enough, you'll let *God* down?

Because we live in a world that is ignorant of the work of God, we overestimate the work of humanity. But true Sabbath brings true dignity back to our work because it sees our work for what it is: God-given, proper, and completely unable to give us an identity.

Sabbath is a time of celebrating. It is a time of releasing control. It is a time for remembering that you are not in control.

Perhaps most importantly, Sabbath is a time for renewing your confidence in the truest thing about you. Your core identity. You are not your job. You are not defined by your work. You are not responsible for controlling life.

Sabbath is the way for you to look at your job, your career, and say with glad liberation, *You are great, but you are not my life! Christ is my life, and I am in Christ!*

That is the Sabbath identity from which our workweeks flow. Sabbath is the discipline that both proves we are living in Christ and trains us to live in Christ. It allows us to have rightly ordered enjoyment of the gifts God gives us. Sabbath does not exist for what it gives us, nor for how it helps us, but for the way it equips us to live into our true identities. We are not "human doings," but "human beings."[13]

Let us, as we take Sabbath, become who we are and reject the lie that our worth and our identity come from what we do.

8

GOD WON'T STOP
THE TRUEST TRUTH

*Holiness is love locked into the True Center, Jesus Christ
our Lord. Being "true," all of the self—and progressively all
of life—comes into harmony and wholeness and strength.*

Mildred Wynkoop, *A Theology of Love*

JESUS LOSES HIS MOJO

Right in the middle of the gospel of Mark we read a story
that is found nowhere else—perhaps because no other
gospel writer was brave enough to include it! It's the story
of Jesus working a miracle that doesn't quite work. At least
not at first.

This takes place in the town of Bethsaida. Some people bring a blind man to Jesus, knowing that if Jesus can simply touch the blind man, he will be healed. We don't know if the people are the blind man's relatives or neighbors. Perhaps the blind man is a drain on their village's collective time and energy, and they simply want him to start pulling his weight. At last the blind man's escorts succeed in getting him close to Jesus. Mission accomplished—He'll take over from here on out.

But then Jesus starts to act a little oddly. Instead of healing the blind man right then and there, Jesus takes him by the hand and leads him outside the town. Once they're alone, or at least *more* alone than they were in the center of town, Jesus does something even stranger.

He spits in the blind man's eyes.

Jesus can heal any way He wants, so why choose this way? We're not told. But we *are* told that Jesus asks a follow-up question: "Do you see anything?"[1]

Now *that* might be the weirdest part of a bizarre story. It surprises me every time I read it. You'd think that if someone were capable of working miracles, like Jesus was, then He'd be the first to know whether the miracle *took*, so to speak. Why does Jesus have to check with His patient?

The blind man replies honestly: "I see people; they look like trees walking around."[2]

Now we know this isn't Middle-earth, so the man isn't seeing Ents walking around. What he's seeing are people, but he isn't seeing them clearly. It's almost as if Jesus is unsuccessful in His attempt to cure the man—like He gets the miracle partway but not all the way right. The healing worked because the man went from blind to sighted, but the healing also did not work because the man could not see clearly.

So Jesus tries again. He goes back for a second round of healing. This is the only time we read about Jesus doing a miracle in stages, which begs an obvious question.

Why?

MORE CHANGE THAN WE EXPECT

We're given new identities, and then God works in us according to His purpose, without ever giving up or stopping before the job is finished.

The difficulty is that we need to change a great deal more than we think.

We may think we have one problem to tackle, one habit or character flaw to overcome. God, however, isn't after improvement—He's after much more. Let me explain.

We often meet God for the first time because of our desire for partial transformation. And that's not a bad thing. It's wonderful, in fact. Say someone is fired from the only job she could find, and in despair she turns to God for help. Or someone is abused by another person, and because he cannot turn to anyone else, he turns to God.

And God meets those people! They experience a definite improvement. Perhaps a community of Christians helps the person who was fired pay rent or find a new job. Perhaps God gives the person who was abused a certainty that he is loved and protected. Like the blind man in Mark 8, they go from darkness to light. For the first time in their lives they can *see* something.

However, while God meets us in our place of need, He is after something beyond that particular need. God wants *complete* regeneration. *Complete* transformation. Not just improvement.

We want to overcome a single destructive relationship, but God wants to bring our entire sexuality in line with His purposes. God wants to transform not just the way we interact with men, or women, but with *all* people. God wants to remake our understanding of relationships, to change the way we approach lovers and friends and strangers.

Or *we* want to beat a single addiction, but *God* wants to reorient the way we interact with every substance. Not just alcohol or drugs, but everything we consume. God wants to show us how we are connected to one another and to the earth by what we eat and how we eat it.

We want to reprioritize so that we don't get our identity from overworking, but *God* wants to show us that nothing in life can bring us the pleasure and joy of knowing Him. God wants to restore our sense of Sabbath, to bring us to a reimagined understanding of our role as doers and workers in His creation.

God's vision always goes beyond ours. We are often pursuing the renewal of our circumstances, but God is pursuing the renewal of our entire identity. Think of the Sermon on the Mount: Jesus didn't give us arbitrary rules but rather offered a way forward into holistic transformation. The point is not to simply get rid of anger, but to move beyond anger and into love and forgiveness, even of our enemies.

Have you ever been at a restaurant and seen a mother trying to clean her young child's face? Small kids have a knack for getting part of everything they eat smeared and stuck on their cheeks: ketchup, melted cheese, bits of hamburger, and even a streak of snot for good measure. The kids generally do *not* want their faces cleaned, but Mom always wins. With one hand she holds her child's head so he can't squirm away, while the other hand dips a napkin into the closest glass of water. (Don't forget, Mom will even lick the closest napkin if she needs to.) Then comes the wipe: deliberate, repeatedly targeted, thorough. Kids are unhappy every time. They're often preverbal, but what they're communicating is loud and clear. *Mom, why are you abusing me? Why are you making a scene? Can't you see I don't* want *my face cleaned?*

Yes, she can! But Mom goes after the kid over and over anyway, until she sees a clean face.

That's exactly what God does with us.

I've experienced it time and time again. He wants to clean me off, restore my image, and every time I pull away. Every time I tell God that I don't need to be cleaned, that I've already cleaned up enough. And every time God is like, *Dave, I'm doing you a favor here. Despite what you'd like to think, you don't look attractive with that ketchup smeared all over your face. Or the melted cheese. Now let's get back to work and get you all the way clean.*

We need to trust that God is working in us, that He will bring His work to completion, and that He's working all this for our good and His glory.

And we need to know that it might take longer than we thought.

"ONCE MORE"

So what does all this have to do with a partially healed blind man?

After the man tells Jesus that all he can see are trees walking around, the story tells us that "once more" Jesus puts His hands on the man.

There may be two reasons for this. One is that Jesus is going to try to heal the man again—more on that in a moment. The other reason is one I can't prove but I suspect may be true. Imagine you're the man. You've just been taken by a group of people to a strange town. You've been introduced to Jesus, and Jesus has taken you outside the town, leading you by the hand. Jesus has spit into your eyes and touched your eyes. And then you can see! Not perfectly, no, but it's a whole lot better than what you had. Darkness has become shapes and colors. So what do you do? You start to walk away because you're satisfied! You were blind; now you can see. Imperfectly, but you can see.

Then Jesus stops you. Jesus isn't satisfied.

Jesus lays His hands on the man again. And *this* time when he opens his eyes, his sight is restored and he sees *everything* clearly. No more people who look like walking trees ... now people look the way they are meant to look.

I was being provocative earlier when I mentioned that maybe Jesus had lost His mojo. He could, of course, have healed the blind man all at once, just as He could have healed him without touching his eyes or spitting. We need to ask, then, what might have motivated Jesus to take this stage-by-stage approach.

I believe the answer has to do with His disciples—and with us.

Leading up to this healing, Mark told the story in a very particular way. One reason I love Mark's gospel is that he wasn't afraid to point out how dense everyone is—how they can see *some* things but not everything. If there is one thing Mark made clear, it was that proximity to Jesus did not guarantee clear perception. Earlier in Mark, the disciples saw Jesus feed thousands of people with only a tiny amount of bread and fish. They watched Jesus walk on water and calm a storm. Then they saw Jesus *again* feed thousands of people with only a tiny amount of bread and fish.

They *saw* all this, but they didn't yet see Jesus clearly.

They *saw*, but they didn't *see*.

So it is with us.

We, like the disciples, can be right next to Jesus and still not *truly* see Him. We can go to church for decades and still see trees walking upside down.

Our spiritual vision is not healed in an instant, after which we see everything clearly. God. Life. The Bible. Relationships. Church. Family. Career. No, it's a process of prayer, reading, living, reflecting, being discipled, meditating, and experiencing the goodness and relentlessness of God.

We, along with the disciples, might *see* that Jesus is in our lives, but we don't really know what that means. We see the fact without seeing the significance of the fact.

Later in Mark's story, Peter saw a bit more clearly, at least for a moment. Just after the healing of the blind man, Jesus asked His disciples who they thought He was. And it was Peter, of course, always willing to lead the charge, who provided the answer: "You are the Messiah."[3] Peter nailed it! High fives, kisses, hugs, confetti falling from the sky! Jesus has many roles—healer, preacher, teacher, provocateur—but all of these are outworkings of His *identity* as the Messiah and the Son of God.

If we identify with Peter, we can feel pretty good at this point. Like we're finally seeing clearly.

The next passage in Mark puts us right back where we started, however. When Jesus told His disciples that He must suffer and be killed, once again it was Peter who jumped in, rebuking Jesus. We can imagine what he might have said. *That's crazy talk, Jesus—since You're the Messiah, You've come to conquer, not to die!*

Jesus offered a rebuke of His own to Peter, calling His friend "Satan." Peter, because he could not see clearly the full identity of Jesus, could not conceive how suffering fit into the picture.

Peter saw, but he didn't see.

That's us. We're like the blind man after his first encounter with Jesus. We're looking around at our lives, grateful that we can see *something*, even if everyone looks like a walking tree. We might even be content with that. It's a vast improvement over who we used to be, after all.

This book may have helped you see your identity more clearly, or the identity of Jesus more clearly, but you're not there yet. Neither am I.

God won't stop until we can see everything clearly. When we place our trust in Christ, our healing begins. We start to see. But often *we* are satisfied with the quality of our vision long before God is.

So God touches us, again and again, until at last we can see as we were meant to see.

BEAUTIFUL TENSION

God won't stop with partial transformation.

But to what end is God working? What are we being transformed *into*?

God's will is to work in us a character of love and joy and peace and patience and kindness and goodness and faithfulness and gentleness and self-control. God *is* working that in us—and here's the crazy part, the part I have trouble believing most days:

God will complete that work in me.

There is something so scandalous, so flat-out impossible about that truth that it almost becomes comforting. This is not a truth about God that I would have made up if I'd been in charge of writing the Bible. I would have made the plan something like this: God does something amazing for me, so in return He requires me to do something amazing for Him.

Surely it can't be that God starts by doing something amazing for me and then *keeps* doing something amazing for me.

But Scripture tells us that's precisely what God is doing, no matter how crazy or impossible it sounds. God *is* working in those He has rescued. This is the way Paul staked out the matter, saying he was *sure* of this: *that the One who began a good work in us will bring it to completion.*[4]

And that's the good news right there—that *God* is the One who will bring the work in us to its intended goal. It's not up to us. It isn't about us using our strength or cleverness or dedication to cross the goal line. It's God's responsibility. God's the One working in us, pushing us, and sometimes carrying us. Which is why it's God who controls exactly how much change we go through.

When God changes us, we don't control how much change we go through. God does. He works in us to will and to do according to His purpose, and He will complete His work.

When the blind man received partial sight, Jesus didn't ask him to fix the rest of his vision himself. Jesus touched the man again and accomplished the healing.

....

At the same time, however, we work *out* in our lives what God is working *in* us.

I want to say that again. We work *out* what God is working *in*.

When I first taught this material about identity at my church, my wife was well aware of how it was affecting me. I was more tempted, more vulnerable, more melancholy than she'd ever seen me before. At the same time, I was more excited, more high, more filled with passion and fire than she'd ever seen me before. It was more difficult for me to hear God, but when I did, it seemed like God was speaking directly to me. It was harder to focus on studying and taking notes, but there were times when it felt like I was seeing right to the heart of life.

One morning, before I left our house, my wife asked me to sit down so she could pray for me. It was an ordinary morning—both of us headed out to work in the city, both of us thinking of our to-do lists for the day—but what she said was so extraordinary in its insight that I can still hear her word for word.

God, these last three months that Dave has been wrestling with this stuff and just getting destroyed by it—God, maybe that's just simply the tension between how You're working in, God, and how Dave is working it out.

If you'd been watching us that morning, as we sat there on the couch holding hands and bowing our heads, you would have seen one of those cartoon lightbulbs appear above my head. *Click!* The minute my wife prayed that, it all made sense. I'd been feeling like I was walking the edge of a precipice, close to falling off into a pit of contradiction.

On the one hand, our new identity is given to us by God, and it is God who is at work in us and who never stops.

On the other hand, we aren't passive bystanders who begin to live righteous and godly lives with no effort.

But my wife's prayer showed me that I wasn't about to fall into the valley of contradiction—far from it! Rather, a sense of peace flooded over me, washing me in the knowledge that I was living and studying and preaching in the middle of a *creative tension*.

God is at work in me, and I work out my own salvation.

I contribute nothing to my own salvation, yet as I work it out, God is working in me.

These are creative tensions. Beautiful tensions. We can feel a sort of holy awe when we see that God has chosen, and is choosing, to work His perfect will in us and through us.

We are partial people. Incomplete people. But God won't stop.

TRIALS

God is working into you His will, according to His pleasure, and He's not pleased to stop with one sin or one flaw or one bad habit.

God is after total restoration.

After partially healing the blind man, Jesus could have stopped. Here is a man who's moved from complete blindness to being able to recognize people walking past him. He'll be able to work a trade now and earn some income. Maybe he'll find a wife and have some kids. He might never pass a twenty-twenty vision test, but he'll see the colors of the sunset and the smile on the face of a friend.

Except that Jesus isn't finished. Jesus has the man close his eyes, and then Jesus touches the man's eyes a second time. When the man opens his eyes, the tree people have been replaced by real people. The blind man can't just see better after his encounter with Jesus—he can see everything clearly.

I have to trust that God is always working in me and that He won't stop, because bringing about total restoration is going to take a lifetime and beyond.

That sort of trust seems achievable in those moments when I happen to agree with what God is working on. If I want to beat my alcohol problem, and God is working to help me beat my alcohol problem, it's relatively easy to trust God through those trials and suffering. I can justify it by telling myself, *No pain, no gain.* God and I are on the same page.

The trick is believing that God is after my good when I'm not on board with His project. When I'm in for an ounce, and He's in for a pound, it can feel like I'm being punished for something. Trust can quickly decay during times of suffering and uncertainty, leading me not just to question if God is working, but to question whether He's actually working for my downfall.

Here's the truth about that, however: God's work in my life is "*never* punitive and *always* redemptive."[5]

Does that sound like good news? Or news that's too good to be true? Nevertheless, Scripture is crystal clear about this point. If we've been rescued by God, God doesn't punish us for our sins. God doesn't punish us in wrath. Period. The reason is this: there is no wrath for our sins left. Jesus absorbed every ounce on the cross, once and literally for all.[6]

This means that when something bad happens to me—from missing the bus and being late to work all the way to getting cancer or losing a spouse—I can remove the question "Why is God punishing me?" from the situation. God is not *punishing* me, because when God looks at me He sees a perfectly righteous and perfectly lived life, thanks to what Jesus did on my behalf.

Instead God is working to transform me, and God doesn't stop.

I believe this, but I don't always trust it.

I still wrestle with this when things go south in my life. *What did I do to deserve this? Did I not pray enough? Was I too proud or too angry or too selfish? Not disciplined enough?* No. The gospel is called good news for a reason. We aren't stuck on a karmic treadmill. We don't get what we deserve. God doesn't backhand us when He wakes up on the wrong side of the bed.

Jesus covers us. Completely. All that's left is redemption—and redemption is the process of God *willing* and *doing* what is necessary to completely transform us.

What if, when your career suddenly ends, God isn't punishing but redeeming? What if, when a relationship collapses, God isn't punishing but redeeming? What if, when the doctors say you can't have kids, God isn't punishing but redeeming?

I don't write this flippantly. I've experienced difficult, heartbreaking things in my life, and I've walked with friends who have experienced infinitely more difficulty and heartbreak. Life can feel unbelievably hard. It can feel like it will crush us. It can feel like God is crushing us.

But when our lives are hidden with Christ in God, we are not crushed. The apostle Paul had a physical ailment, and he asked God to remove it and make him whole. He asked again and again, and each time God told Paul that his ailment was bringing about redemption. It was God working for good in Paul's life, and Paul needed to trust that.

Not just believe it—*trust* it.

Paul was intimately acquainted with suffering when he wrote that "we are hard pressed on every side, but not crushed; perplexed, but not in despair; persecuted, but not abandoned; struck down, but not destroyed. We always carry around in our body the death of Jesus, so that the life of Jesus may also be revealed in our body. For we who are alive are always being given over to death for Jesus' sake, so that his life may also be revealed in our mortal body."[7]

Paul also knew that God's grace is sufficient for us in this life and that God's power is made perfect in our weakness. And *that* is a reason to boast! We can be proud when we suffer, as strange as that sounds, because those are the times when God's grace and power are demonstrated most clearly in our lives. It won't be easy, but it will be good.

God is at work in us. God will continue that work until we are completely transformed. God will lay hands on us time and again until we realize complete restoration.

Wait, we protest, *that will take forever!*

And?

TRUST

Here we are, at the end of the book. And this is the question I want to leave you with.

What is our part in working out all this identity talk?

Trust.

Remember the tightrope walker Blondin? Let me invite you into a similar story—a way to see the shape of trust that is *lived*.

Imagine I'm a world-class knife thrower, and you've traveled from a neighboring town to see me perform. You stand in line, you plunk down your money at the door, and you find a seat close to the front. The lights dim, a hush falls over the audience, and suddenly I stride onto the stage. After shrugging my cape to the floor, I hold up my arms and announce that I'm going to perform feats of dexterity and daring such as you've never imagined. (I'll admit, I'm having fun imagining this.)

To begin my performance, I attach a dummy to a vertical wheel and step back twenty paces. Then I call for my beautiful assistant, who sashays over to the wheel and spins it. After a dramatic pause, my right arm becomes a blur as I launch three slim knives toward the target—*thwick thwick thwick*! My assistant stops the wheel to reveal the three knives embedded in a tight halo around the dummy's head. I turn and bow, and after a slight pause, the audience erupts in cheers.

When the applause dies down, I let the silence hang for a moment. Then I ask a simple question: "Do you *believe* I can do this with a live volunteer?"

"Yes!" roars the audience, and you join in.

"Would you like to see it?"

The roar is even louder this time. You're cheering along, excited and partly terrified to see the lovely assistant step up to the wheel and allow herself to be strapped down. I shout my third question over the buzz of the crowd.

"And who volunteers?"

Total silence. All eyes hit the floor. All eyes except yours—you were too shocked by my question to look down in time. Now we're making eye contact.

You *believe* I can perform this feat with a live person—but does your belief extend to *trust*? Will your belief become *action*? Those questions will be answered clearly in the next thirty seconds as you decide whether to remain in your seat or to gather your courage and walk toward the stage.

Belief might lead to trust, and belief might even get you out of your seat, but the question remains:

Will you trust?

In this book, I *may* have presented a compelling case for you to think differently about your identity. But believing it is different than trusting it.

Believing it might lead you to quote this book, tell others about it, feel better about your life, or even go back to church.

But that doesn't mean you trust.

Sometimes we believe God is working in us. Sometimes we believe God will continue to work in us until the job is finished. Sometimes we even believe that God knows best—that His plan for our restoration and transformation is the right one.

But what does it look like for you to *trust* those things?

At this point in the book you might expect application points. A "to-do list" of identity. Some journal questions. Five things you can do in the next five weeks to actualize your new identity.

But that's not what this book is about. Unless you drive the single message of this book to the core of your being—beyond belief, to the place of your deepest trust—no application will stick.

So here it is.

You will not find your identity in what you have, but in who has you. You will not find your identity in what you do, but in what has been done for you. And you will not find your identity in what you desire, but in who has desired—at infinite cost to Himself—a relationship with you.

Christ is your life. He gives you a new identity and will work that new identity out in your life until the day when He appears. On that day you will finally see clearly, as Christ sees you now. You will know as you are known.

And you will understand that the truest thing about you—that *in Christ* God called you His beloved in whom He is well pleased—has been true all along.

And is now true forever.

Believe. Trust. Base your entire identity and worth on that fact.

ACKNOWLEDGMENTS

First I'd like to thank Britt Merrick for calling me after my first sermon in the identity series in 2011 and saying that this topic needed to be my first book, and then being such an encourager through the whole process. I'd like to thank my friends and family at Reality San Francisco for taking this journey with me into the truest thing about us ... and we continue to journey. To the staff at RSF, there are no other people I'd rather be doing life and ministry with. And Tarik, thank you for everything—too much to name here, brother. To the team at David C Cook, for putting up with me and my thousand-plus changes during the course of this project and for being the absolute best team of people to work with. To my family, my mom and dad for your support and keeping me grounded the whole time. To David Jacobsen, thank you, my friend—this book wouldn't be what it is without all your hard work, care, and intelligence. To Dann Petty for helping this book look so dang good. To Nicci Hubert for taking some major editing risks that paid off big-time. To Don Jacobson for holding my hand through this whole process and being my advocate and coach throughout. To Francis Chan for the beautiful foreword and for being such a good friend and mentor to me in SF. To Tim Chaddick for allowing me to call during every one of my own personal identity crises and to hear on the other line, "Me, too!"—a true friend. And to Ashley, for knowing me and my flaws for twenty years and loving me anyway. I love you.

NOTES

FOREWORD

1. Matthew 7:17–20
2. Luke 6:45
3. Ezekiel 36:26
4. Romans 8:9–39
5. Romans 6:17–18

CHAPTER 1: WHO WE ARE

1. John 6:55
2. Proverbs 31
3. Mitch Wasden, "Why an Identity Crisis Might Be Just What Your Brain Needs," HBR Blog Network, November 23, 2011, http://blogs.hbr.org/cs/2011/11/why_an_identity_crisis_might_b.html.

CHAPTER 2: HOW WE GOT HERE

1. Jonathan Franzen, *Freedom* (New York: Farrar, Straus and Giroux, 2010), 432.

2. This question is taken from Soma Communities, *The Storyformed Way Leaders' Guide*, http://www.gcmcollective.org/article/story-formed-way/.

3. Bureau of Labor Statistics, Economic News Release, "America's Young Adults at 25," March 1, 2013, http://www.bls.gov/news.release/nlsyth.nr0.htm.

4. Joshua Knobe, "In Search of the True Self," *New York Times*, June 5, 2011, http://opinionator.blogs.nytimes.com/2011/06/05/in-search-of-the-true-self/.

5. Knobe, "In Search of the True Self."

6. Jenell Williams Paris, *The End of Sexual Identity* (Downers Grove, IL: InterVarsity Press, 2011), 56.

7. Paris, *The End of Sexual Identity*, 75.

8. Ronald Rolheiser, *The Holy Longing* (New York: Doubleday, 1999), 7.

9. Paris, *The End of Sexual Identity*, 10.

10. Paris, *The End of Sexual Identity*, 57.

11. This idea was taken from Paris, *The End of Sexual Identity*, 106–107.

12. I'm defining the gospel here in the way Timothy Keller simply but profoundly put it: Religion says, "I obey; therefore, I am accepted by God." Gospel says, "I am accepted by God through Christ; therefore, I obey."

13. Bruce K. Waltke, *An Old Testament Theology* (Grand Rapids: Zondervan, 2007), 211.

CHAPTER 3: WHAT WE ARE MEANT TO BE

1. To explain the Trinity would be outside the scope of this work. Wayne Grudem said, "The biblical teaching on the Trinity tells us that all of God's attributes are true of all three persons, for each is fully God. Thus, God the Son and God the Holy Spirit are also eternal [with God the Father], omnipresent, omnipotent, infinitely wise, infinitely holy, infinitely loving, omniscient, and so forth." (Grudem, *Systematic Theology* [Leicester, Great Britain: Inter-Varsity Press, 1994], 226)

2. Genesis 1:26. Though the New International Version, which is quoted here, uses the word *mankind* instead of *human*, I have used *human* throughout to reflect the intent of the original language to include both male and female in the context.

3. Genesis 1:27

4. Though our fundamental identity did not change at the fall, it was marred. Only Jesus can restore us to our true identity, as we will see.

5. Beyoncé, "Single Ladies," *I Am … Sasha Fierce* © 2008 Columbia.

6. A nod to Tim Keller for pointing this out.

7. Genesis 1:27

8. Matthew 25:40

9. Romans 3:23

10. 1 Timothy 2:4

11. John 1:1–4

12. Genesis 2:18

13. Simon & Garfunkel,"I Am a Rock," *Sounds of Silence* © 1966 Columbia.

14. Eugene H. Peterson, *First and Second Samuel* (Louisville, KY: Westminster John Knox Press, 1999), 101.

15. J. R. R. Tolkien, "On Fairy-Stories," 14, public.callutheran.edu/~brint/Arts/Tolkien.pdf.

16. Ecclesiastes 3:11

17. C. S. Lewis, *The Problem of Pain* (New York: HarperOne, 2001), 116.

18. Eben Alexander, *Proof of Heaven* (New York: Simon & Schuster, 2012), 39.

19. Colossians 1:15

20. John 14:7

21. Hebrews 1:3

CHAPTER 4: THE TRUEST HUMAN

1. Bruce K. Waltke, *An Old Testament Theology* (Grand Rapids: Zondervan, 2007), 211.

2. Dale S. Kuehne, *Sex and the iWorld* (Grand Rapids: Baker, 2009), 139.

3. Kuehne, *Sex and the iWorld*, 140.

4. Matthew 3:14, author's paraphrase

5. Matthew 3:15

6. Matthew 3:17, author's paraphrase

7. Hebrews 1:3

8. Hebrews 13:8

9. Ephesians 1:4 NASB

10. Matthew 3:17

11. David G. Benner, *Surrender to Love* (Downers Grove, IL: InterVarsity Press, 2003),

12. A phrase I stole from my friend Jon Tyson.

13. Annie Dillard, *Teaching a Stone to Talk* (New York: HarperCollins, 1992), 32.

14. John 13:3

15. Matthew 3:17 NASB

16. Matthew 27:46

17. Frederick Dale Bruner, *Matthew: A Commentary, Volume 2: The Churchbook, Matthew 13–28* (Grand Rapids: Eerdmans, 2004), 746.

18. Bruner, *Matthew*, 746.

19. Bruner, *Matthew*, 746.

CHAPTER 5: OUR HUMAN CONDITION

1. C. S. Lewis, *The Voyage of the Dawn Treader* (New York: HarperCollins, 1994), 91.

2. John Mayer, "New Deep," *Heavier Things* © 2003 Columbia.

3. Lewis, *The Voyage of the Dawn Treader*, 108.

4. C. S. Lewis, *The Lion, the Witch and the Wardrobe* (New York: HarperCollins, 1994), 86.

5. Lewis, *The Voyage of the Dawn Treader*, 108.

6. Psalm 139; Ephesians 1:4–10

7. Lewis, *The Voyage of the Dawn Treader*, 109.

8. Lewis, *The Voyage of the Dawn Treader*, 109.

9. Lewis, *The Voyage of the Dawn Treader*, 110.

CHAPTER 6: OUR GREATEST HOPE

1. Matthew 16:24–25

2. C. S. Lewis, *Mere Christianity* (New York: HarperCollins, 2000), 227.

3. Colossians 2:21

4. Colossians 2:23

5. Tim Keller, *Gospel Christianity: Course 3* (New York: Redeemer Presbyterian Church, 2003), 141.

6. Sinclair Ferguson, "Our Holiness: The Father's Purpose and the Son's Purchase" (sermon, Banner of Truth Conference, Grantham, PA, May 29, 2007).

7. Exodus 20:2

8. Matthew 3:17 NASB

9. John 8:1–11

10. Henri J. Nouwen, *Life of the Beloved* (New York: Crossroad, 1992), 25–33.

11. Adapted from Lewis, *Mere Christianity.*

CHAPTER 7: A WAY FORWARD

1. I got some of this from a class taught by Bill Clem; the rest I added myself.

2. Exodus 20:2

3. 1 Corinthians 1:2; translation from Jerry Breshears.

4. Roy E. Ciampa and Brian S. Rosner, *The Pillar New Testament Commentary: The First Letter to the Corinthians* (Grand Rapids: Eerdmans, 2010), 50.

5. Kwame Anthony Appiah, *The Ethics of Identity* (Princeton, NJ: Princeton University Press, 2005), 17.

6. Eugene L. Lowry, *The Homiletical Plot* (Louisville, KY: Westminster John Knox Press, 2001), 64.

7. Colossians 1:20

8. Blaise Pascal, *Pensées*, 417, trans. A. J. Krailsheimer (New York: Penguin Classics, 1995), 121.

9. 1 Corinthians 7:29–30

10. Mark Buchanan, *The Rest of God* (Nashville: Thomas Nelson, 2006), 87.

11. Eugene H. Peterson, *Working the Angles* (Grand Rapids: Eerdmans, 1987), 67.

12. Peterson, *Working the Angles*, 66.

13. Peter Scazzero, *The Emotionally Healthy Church*, updated and expanded ed. (Grand Rapids: Zondervan, 2010), 34.

CHAPTER 8: GOD WON'T STOP

1. Mark 8:23

2. Mark 8:24

3. Mark 8:29

4. Philippians 1:6

5. Elyse Fitzpatrick, *Because He Loves Me* (Wheaton, IL: Crossway, 2008), 88.

6. 2 Corinthians 4:8–11

7. 2 Corinthians 4:8–11